ROUTLEDGE LIBRARY EDITIONS:
MANAGEMENT

Volume 49

MANAGERIAL PLANNING

MANAGERIAL PLANNING
An Optimum and Stochastic Control Approach
(Volume One)

CHARLES S. TAPIERO

LONDON AND NEW YORK

First published in 1977 by Gordon and Breach Science Publishers, Inc.

This edition first published in 2018
by Routledge
2 Park Square, Milton Park, Abingdon, Oxon OX14 4RN

and by Routledge
711 Third Avenue, New York, NY 10017

Routledge is an imprint of the Taylor & Francis Group, an informa business

© 1977 Gordon and Breach Science Publishers, Inc.

All rights reserved. No part of this book may be reprinted or reproduced or utilised in any form or by any electronic, mechanical, or other means, now known or hereafter invented, including photocopying and recording, or in any information storage or retrieval system, without permission in writing from the publishers.

Trademark notice: Product or corporate names may be trademarks or registered trademarks, and are used only for identification and explanation without intent to infringe.

British Library Cataloguing in Publication Data
A catalogue record for this book is available from the British Library

ISBN: 978-1-138-55938-7 (Set)
ISBN: 978-1-351-05538-3 (Set) (ebk)
ISBN: 978-0-8153-6582-2 (Volume 49) (hbk)
ISBN: 978-1-351-26052-7 (Volume 49) (ebk)

Publisher's Note
The publisher has gone to great lengths to ensure the quality of this reprint but points out that some imperfections in the original copies may be apparent.

Disclaimer
The publisher has made every effort to trace copyright holders and would welcome correspondence from those they have been unable to trace.

Managerial Planning

An Optimum and Stochastic Control Approach

VOLUME ONE

Charles S. Tapiero

GORDON AND BREACH   New York London Paris

Copyright © 1977 by Gordon and Breach Science Publishers, Inc.

Gordon and Breach Science Publishers, Inc.
One Park Avenue
New York, NY10016

Gordon and Breach Science Publishers Ltd.
42 William IV Street
London WC2N 4DF

Gordon & Breach
7-9 rue Emile Dubois
Paris 75014

Library of Congress catalog card number 77-77587
ISBN 0 677 05400 9
All rights reserved. No part of this book may be reproduced or utilized in any form or by any means, electronic or mechanical including photocopying, recording, or by any information storage and retrieval system, without permission in writing from the publishers. Printed in Great Britain.

à maman

TABLE OF CONTENTS

Volume 1

Foreword	xi
Acknowledgement	xiii
Preface	xv

CHAPTER I: ON TIME		1
I.1	Introduction	1
I.2	Time and Management	3
I.3	Modeling Time Related Activities	18
I.4	Decision Making and Decision Criteria	27
I.5	Time and Operational Models	35
I.6	Summary	45
	Footnotes	46
	References	49
	Problems	53
CHAPTER II: PLANNING AND PLANNING MODELS - OVER TIME		55
II.1	A Classification of Planning Activities	56
II.2	Quantification of Memory Processes; (1) No memory, (2) Differential Memory, (3) Delay Memory, (4) Integro-differential Memory, (5) Anticipative Memory	66
II.3	Memory Processes - Mathematical Examples	76
II.4	Probabilistic Memory - Stochastic Processes; (1) Properties of Stochastic Processes, (2) Random Walks, (3) The Wiener-Levy Process (or Brownian Motion), (4) The Markov Process, (5) The Poisson Process, (6) Stochastic Integrals and Stochastic Differential Equations	84
II.5	Applications	108
II.6	Discounting; (1) Probabilistic Discount Rates, (2) The Probability Distribution of Consumers' Discount Rates, (3) The Probability Distribution of a Consumers' Discount Rates in Acquiring a New Car	121
	Footnotes	139
	References	143
	Problems	148

Appendices		159
1: Differential Equation		159
2: Stochastic Calculus		165

CHAPTER III: PLANNING DECISION--OVER TIME 172

III.1	Introduction	172
III.2	Control Systems - Over Time (1) Deterministic Control Problems, (2) Estimation, (3) Stochastic Control, (4) Identification, (5) Adaptive Control, (6) Inverse Control	173
III.3	Applications	198
III.4	Information Control	218
III.5	The Choice of Decision Struqtures	226
	Footnotes	230
	References	232
	Problems	238

Volume 2

Preface to the Second Volume ix

CHAPTER IV: OPTIMIZATION UNDER CERTAINTY 241

IV.1	Introduction	241
IV.2	Discrete Time Optimization - An Overview; (1) Classical Optimization Procedure, (2) Calculus of Variations Procedure, (3) The Control Procedure, (4) The Dynamic Programming Procedure	243
IV.3	The Calculus of Variations (1) Euler's Necessary Conditions for Optimality, (2) Special Cases, (3) Special Forms of Euler's Necessary Conditions	256
IV.4	Optimum Control and the Maximum Principle (1) The Maximum Principle - Statement, (2) Comparison Between the Variational Approach and Dynamic Programming	269
IV.5	Special Cases; (1) Optimization of Parameters, (2) Time Delays, (3) Decision Timing	287

IV.6	Miscellaneous Applications	301
	Footnotes	326
	References	329
	Problems	341
	Appendices	353
	1: Classical Optimization - A Survey	354
	2: Continuous Functional Perturbation - Euler's Equation	361
	3: Sufficiency Conditions and Second Variations	363
	4: Canonical Form of The Calculus of Variations	365
	5: The Continuous Time Maximum Principle	368
	6: The Discrete Time Maximum Principle	375
	7: The Multivariate Quadratic Cost Linear Control Problem	383
	8: Performance Sensitivity	385
	9: Necessary Conditions for Optimum Control with Time Delays	386
	10: Controllability and Observability	389

CHAPTER V: ESTIMATION HYPOTHESIS TESTING AND OPTIMIZATION 391

   V.1 Introduction 391

   V.2 Evolution of Stochastic Models - Deterministic Realizations; 396
(1) The Transform Approach, (2) The Bayes Approach,
(3) Nonlinear Models

   V.3 Estimation and Identification; 419
(1) Estimation of Linear Models, (2) Nonlinear Models and
Filtering, (3) Identification and Adaptive Filtering

   V.4 Hypothesis Testing 459

   V.5 Optimization; 466
(1) Deterministic Equivalents, (2) Stochastic Dynamic Programming,
(3) Stochastic Maximum Principle.

   V.6 Miscellaneous Applications and Extensions 489

      Footnotes 511

      References 515

      Problems 530

      Appendices 545
      1: Nonlinear Identification in Continuous
         Time - A Maximum Likelihood Approach
      2: The Log Likelihood Ratio of Two Competing Hypotheses

CHAPTER VI: SIMULATION AND NUMERICAL METHODS 549

   VI.1 Introduction 549

   VI.2 Definition of Simulation 551

   VI.3 Simulation Time Related Activities 557

VI.4	Applications	569
VI.5	Simulation & Languages; (1) Dynamo, (2) CSMP	581
VI.6	Numerical Methods; (1) Linear Programming, (2) Dynamic Programming; (3) Finite Difference Approximations, (4) The Method of Gradients, (5) Newton Raphson Methods	590
	Footnotes	603
	Problems	604
	References	607
	Appendices 1: Subroutines 2: Computer Programs	613 613 614
	Author Index	629
	Subject Index	635

Foreword

The essence of planning is embodied in the temporal dimension. Yet much is written about planning with only vague references to the constraints imposed by timing and the opportunities that time alone allows.

Time is the dominant variable where change is sought. New objectives become feasible as the planning horizon increases. Planning horizons are intimately connected with personal attitudes and subjective perceptions. Can it be that through time considerations we can begin to merge behavioral realities with quantitative modeling?

Reading Charles Tapiero's book, I think you will agree with me, he has shown that many potential connections exist. Professor Tapiero has elevated time to the critically important systems parameter that it deserves to be. Where he uses time as an important control model variable, he avoids the trap of narrowing rather than expanding the scope of the system. So often, time has been converted to sequence and sequence to constraint, that management scientists tend to flinch and duck when they observe that time consideration has reduced managerial opportunities rather than expanded them.

With this book, **Professor Tapiero,** has succeeded in changing the way in which a system should be studied. He has increased our familiarity with time and has encouraged systems modelers to expand their allowance for interactions not only into the future but also out of the past.

Martin S. Starr
Columbia University

Acknowledgement

In coming to grips with the notion of time, I have benefited from many discussions with my colleagues and friends. Martin K. Starr influenced me to study the implications of managing over time and has given me profound and useful advice throughout my years at Columbia. Donald B. Straus has encouraged and helped me to comprehend managerial perspectives in dealing with complex problems. Paul Kleindorder devoted a great amount of his time to a thorough in-depth review of the book. His suggestions, always appropriate have been included and his contribution is gratefully acknowledged. Esther Tuval, relentlessly, typed this manuscript often under great pressure. Her help and good humor is acknowledged. My greatest debt is to my wife Judy and children Daniel and Dafna. Their help, tolerance of difficult moments, and patience, were instrumental in the completion of this book.

The writing of such a comprehensive book on time and control could not, however, been done without referring and reproducing past work on this subject. In particular, I am grateful to the following authors and publishers for allowing me to reproduce portions of their material:

W. W. Norton & Company Inc., (1970) for a summary of "Diffusion Processes and Optimal Advertising Policy" by John P. Gould, in E.S. Phelps et al., Microeconomic Foundations of Employment and Inflation Theory, pp. 336-368.

K.S. Palda and Prentice Hall for the Table of "Original and Seasonally Adjusted U.S. Monthly Sales and Advertising Expenditures of the Lydia Pinkham Co.," Jan. 1954 - July 1960, in K.S. Palda, The Measurement of Cumulative Advertising Effects, Prentice Hall 1964.

Academic Press for the theorems on the elements of Stochastic calculus in appendix II.2 reproduced from A.J. Jazwinsky, Stochastic Processes and Filtering Theory, Academic Press 1970.

Management Science, P.R. Kleindorfer, C.H. Kriebel, G.L. Thompson and G.B. Kleindorfer for most of their paper "Discrete Optimal Production Plans", Management Science, 1976, Forthcoming.

G.B. Kleindorfer, P.R. Kleindorfer and G.L. Thompson for their paper "The Discrete Time Maximum Principle" reproduced in Appendix IV.6.

McGraw Hill and A.P. Sage and J.L. Melsa for reproducing their Tables 7.2-2 (p. 268), 7.3-1 (p. 288), 9.2-1 (p. 434) and a summary of their pages 346-351 in, Estimation Theory with Applications to Communications and Control, New York, McGraw Hill, 1971.

Preface

The truism that management is a dynamic process is reflected in three essential functions: management of time, change, and people. Each of these functions entails problems whose origins can be traced to the special character of time and activities that take place over time. The writing of this book was motivated by a desire to focus greater attention on the importance of time in the modeling of socioeconomic and business processes.

A great deal of literature concerned with time and the quantification of activities occurring over time has appeared--philosophers, psychologists, behavioral and organizational scientists, economists, operation-research scientists, engineers, and mathematicians have all encountered special problems when dealing with time. Each discipline has contributed an important and unique point of view. For example, while philosophers and psychologists deal at length with objective and subjective notions of time, engineers take it for granted that activities take place over time and are concerned instead with the manipulation of these processes. Each point of view adds to our understanding of management over time.

Starting with the idea that management involves time in an essential way, I have attempted to devise methods for formulating, analyzing, solving, and manipulating problems having to do with time. This book is the result of the attempt to formalize the process of problem formulation and the solution of dynamic problems. For this formalization, the concepts of the systems approach--which consists in defining a set of interacting elements and determining the relationship between them--have been used.

The integration of these concepts provides a framework within which situations where time is an important factor can be understood and manipulated in a practical way.

The aims of this book are as follows:

1. To present intuitive concepts of time, the concepts used in philosophy and psychology; these can help give managers a better understanding of the character of activities that take place over time.

2. To increase awareness of the relevance of these concepts in the modeling of dynamic socioeconomic problems, and to demonstrate by means of applications how such modeling may be conducted.

3. To find methods of evaluating the effects of the past upon the present, the effects of the present upon the future, and how both the present and the future can be "managed." In other words, time is introduced as a specific variable in managerial decision-making processes.

4. To find mechanisms and tools for organizing activities that take place over time, computing the probability that certain events will occur in the future, and quantifying these activities for the purpose of analysis.

5. To prescribe quantitative methods which will help management define courses of action when faced with a particular model of activities that take place over time.

In brief, I am trying to make _operational_ the conventional wisdom that management is a dynamic process. In doing this, I take a view of processes as existing _in time_ and emphasize the need to understand time and to analyze and solve problems in a temporal setting.

This book is divided into two parts:

    Part One   Time
    Part Two   Decision Making Over Time

Part One, Time, consisting of two chapters, deals with the concept of time and the ways in which management could use ideas having to do with time in model construction. For example, memory, defined as a mechanism for reproducing some part of the past as a present instant of time, is applied to problems of production management, advertising, exponential smoothing, forecasting, etc. Other concepts related to time, such as change and value, are also used to develop an approach to the management of time.

Chapter I deals with temporal preference and temporal risk--both of critical importance to managers--and their application to a wide variety of problems. While no actual solutions are proposed, the essential difficulties encountered in quantifying the structure of temporal preference are outlined. For example, while management values the ability to maintain decision-making flexibility over time, this "temporal flexibility" is hardly quantifiable. Other problems associated with discounting mechanisms in expressing the time value of money are also indicated.

In Chapter II we consider an outline of activities that take place over time. Planning problems are shown to be conceptually tractable when a time framework is adopted for them. Not only can we then better understand the meaning of dynamic activities over time, but we can also firmly anchor these problems to quantifiable and resolvable models. The quantitative modeling of such problems appears in Part Two.

Part Two, Decision Making Over Time, is concerned with developing a framework for the modeling and quantification of time-related problems. In other words, a large body of such problems is classified and organized by means of the systems approach. This organization will then help us recognize classes of problems which may be resolved by specific quantitative techniques.

Part Two deals with control, information, and applications of control and information problems in time described in the first part of the book. Control, expressed in the choice of one or several courses of action is shown to give rise to six types of problems: (1) control with a perfectly predictable environment; (2) estimation of time series and probabilistic models in time; (3) control under an uncertain environment; (4) identification; (5) adaptive control; and (6) inverse control. Each of these problems raises different questions which Chapter III attempts to clarify. In addition, the concept of information is discussed. The framework of Bayes' decision-making theory is adopted to evaluate and transform problems that are essentially probabilistic into equivalent deterministic ones.

The first three chapters described so far make the first volume of the book. In the second volume, the quantitative and simulation techniques used to observe and optimize systems in time are introduced.

The importance of the dynamic framework for management--both formal and informal--can hardly be overstated. There are few fields of scientific endeavor in which the systems approach is not or may not be applied. When time is included in the systems approach, the scope and potential of systems tools in modeling, analyzing, resolving, and implementing processes is immeasurably increased.

The applicability of the temporal systems approach, however, entails equally important limitations, which can lead to serious misunderstanding of what the approach is achieving and outright misapplication hidden behind the modeling and mathematical complexities of processes.

The unrealized expectations arising from the temporal systems approach are due to a breakdown in communications between the managers in the field and the systems designers. While managers consistently formulate problems and structures in explicitly static but implicitly dynamic frameworks, designers of temporal systems attempt to render explicit the implicit managerial judgements. As a result, they require commitments and assumptions on the part of management which may not easily be granted. The comparatively new tools required by temporal systems processes are an additional factor in the breakdown of communications, a breakdown which often appears irreparable.

These problems are similar to the difficulties encountered by management in introducing computer technology in informational, administrative, organizational, and productive processes. Introducing a <u>dynamic management technology</u> to replace current static management technologies can be expected to generate frictions and difficulties in adjustment. But the appearance of computers in many areas of industry, government, and business, and their undeniable successes, are evidence of their contribution and acceptability; and it may be predicted that dynamic management technology will also gain acceptance.

Advantages and limitations of the temporal systems approach are summarized in the table below; these include only a few of the dimensions which may be useful in evaluating the desirability of a temporal systems approach. The overall advantage of the approach is that we can conceive change, in terms of modeling, and incorporate it in our system studies. This perspective of time will then lead to added dimensions in the analysis of socioeconomic managerial processes.

Temporal Systems Approach

Advantages	Limitations
A powerful conceptualization tool. Provides a dynamic view of dynamic phenomena.	Requires large quantities of data to model the dynamic process empircally.
A systematic approach to the modeling and analysis of processes.	Is mathematically difficult to apply. Numerical methods are complex, requiring considerable computing time and memory
Renders implicit managerial temporal judgements explicit	Is difficult to convey; requires appropriate theoretical training. Only relatively simple processes may be derived and applied.
Is nonmyopic; evaluates past, present, and expected future actions and states in a time perspective.	It is difficult to evaluate and compare past, present, and future at a single instant of time. States are not always easily comparable.

This book may be used for two purposes:

1. It may be used as a whole or in part for courses in operations control and managment planning for business and industrial engineering students in their second year of graduate school.

2. It may be used to help managers incorporate *time* in their day-to-day planning decisions. An explicit concern with the effects *of* time and the effects of decisions *over* time will lead to nonmyopic managerial practices in which operating performance is considered in terms of future operating performance, and vice-versa.

The level of mathematical sophistication required is purposely kept as low as possible throughout the book. Certain sections, however, do require the student to have a background in calculus, difference and differential equations, and statistics. Therefore, a two-semester course in probability theory, statistics, calculus, and operations research, as usually given in graduate schools of business, is a prerequisite for a course based on this book. For the student who is not quantitatively oriented, it is suggested that the chapters dealing with optimization of deterministic and stochastic systems might be omitted, and the simulation methods outlined in Chapter VI considered instead.

C.S.T.

PART I: TIME

I returned, and saw under the sun, that the race is not to the swift, nor the battle to the strong, nor yet bread to the wise, nor yet riches to men of understanding, nor yet favour to men of skill; but time and chance happeneth to them all.

<u>Ecclesiastes</u> 9:11

CHAPTER I: On Time

1.1 Introduction

The accelerating rates at which our social and economic environments change compel us not only to cope with change but also to manage it. The management of time and change is, however, a very complex task, requiring that we understand how and why change occurs over time. To do this, it is necessary that we first understand what time is and how social and economic states are interrelated in time: that is, how they are "temporally dependent" on each other. When this is achieved, the functions of management consist in selecting a succession of steps, actions, events, and conditions which will manage time and change to increase the chances that "desirable" outcomes will occur over time.

In the context of time, management is a complex activity which requires that we define a time preference for various _outcomes_; that we define in detail the available _means_ over time; and that these outcomes and means, together with a representation of the process of change over time--i.e., a _model_ explaining how social and economic states change--be used to decide on an effective action. This temporal framework of management is implicit in most managerial decisions; management simultaneously evaluates various desired outcomes and the implicit and explicit costs incurred in reaching these outcomes at a particular time. Because social and economic states are temporally dependent on each other, there must be serious efforts to construct models which can represent accurately the process of change and the implications of managing decisions over time. When we take time into consideration, the questions traditionally of concern to management-- such as _how_, _where_, and _what_--must be augmented by _when_. The explicit

inclusion of time in management processes provides an opportunity for better
modeling of those processes; and although it entails certain pitfalls, these
can be avoided if:

(1) A better understanding of time and processes is achieved.

(2) Appropriate numerical methods are devised for the control
of processes and the solution of problems connected with
processes.

(3) Static management--that is, management assuming temporal
independence of social and economic states--is transformed
smoothly into dynamic management--management assuming
explicitly that social and economic states are temporally
dependent.

Traditionally, management problems were analyzed "statically."[1] Although
problems of a "dynamic" nature attracted much interest, more often than
not these were analyzed intuitively rather than systematically and
rationally. As a result, the study of processes has been meagre, and
comparatively little attention has been given to the formulation of
managerial problems as having to do with phenomena existing over time.

Management *over* time and *of* time introduces certain considerations
which, although accounted for by managerial behavior, need to be made
explicit by the analyst. If this is to be done, the analyst must reach
an understanding of time and determine the models and methods for the
manipulation of processes. In this chapter, psychological and philosophical
notions of time will be correlated to operational notions of time. Such
notions will allow better comprehension of why and how events occur over
time. This is a prerequisite if we are to observe, model and manage
activities as they occur over time.

1.2 Time and Operations Management

It is appropriate to begin with the questions.[2] *What is time?* and *How is time related to operations management?*

We cannot attempt to define *time* here except by *extension*, for *time* itself is an elusive concept. In management over **time**, time will be associated with specific concepts and will be used as an operational term. In this regard, we will use time much as we use spatial coordinates: but time -- the fourth dimension of human experience -- has characteristics and properties unlike those of the three spatial dimensions, which make it a unique variable.

Approaches to the notion of time may be subdivided into two essential groups: (1) those which define "objective time" and (2) those which define "subjective" or "psychological" time. The notion of objective time assumes that time is measurable in terms of temporal milestones, so that there may be quantitative definition for the passage of time. The time-and-motion studies of Frederick Taylor, and his school of management thought in general, are based on such a concept.[3] The notion of subjective or psychological time, on the other hand, can be summarized as being a function of three essential concepts: (1) memory; (2) change; (3) value. These concepts are of particular importance to modeling over time and therefore will be discussed next in greater detail.

(1) Memory

Piaget,[4] whose conclusions are based on experimental studies of children and adults, proposed that the concept of time is tied to *memory* and is connected to our perception and awareness of elapsed time. Thus without memory, there is no perception of time. In management memory is a particularly useful concept,[5] as it is a mechanism for modeling intricate operational processes that exist through time.

Suppose that a system contains an evolution or behavior which is not recorded temporally. Then time as a dimension of analysis is simply not defined. Conversely, unless time-related activities are patterned, or in sequence, memory does not exist.[6] In other words, time and memory are intrinsically related, and both are essential to the modeling of processes. Time is a variable recording the evolution of a process: memory is an incremental description of the evolution of a process over time.

Time and memory, in both the psychological and the operational senses, can also form the basis for distinguishing among past, present, and future. Objectively, the present is simply now; subjectively, the present consists of both the past and the future. This idea has been best stated by Saint Augustine, in his Confessions:

> ...yet perchance it might be properly said, 'there be three times; a present of things past, a present of things present, and a present of things future.' For these three do exist in some sort, in the soul, but otherwhere do I not see them; present of things past, memory; present of things present, sight: present of things future, expectation.[7]

As Figure 1.1 indicates, we always are in the present. But the present has three dimensions:

(1) The present of the past

(2) The present of the present

(3) The present of the future

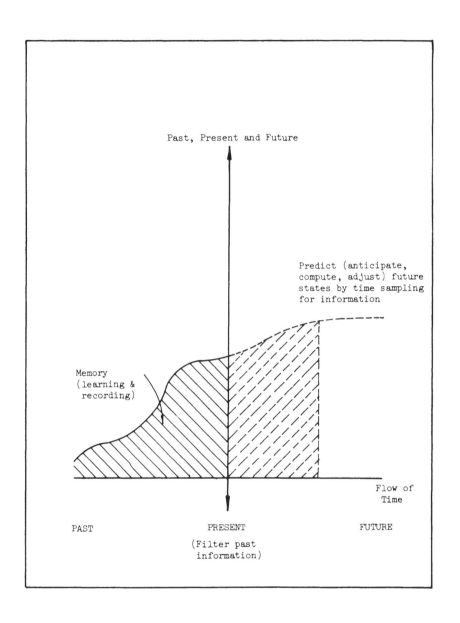

Figure I.1: Past, Present and Future

At any instant of time, our actions depend not only on our current state but on our <u>memory</u> of the past and our anticipation of the future.[8] Some of our actions account for this explicitly; all our actions account for it implicitly. In other words, we may say that each of our acts can be seen in a temporal perspective. Operationally, we construct the past with experiences and empirical observations of temporal processes; our construction of the future, on the other hand, must be in terms of indeterminate and uncertain events which are not always the reflection of the past. We have <u>different mechanisms</u> for establishing opinions of things past and things that may happen in the future. We cannot influence events once they have occurred, but we can influence both their present and their future consequences.[9] We exercise influence by the actions and strategies we adopt as well as by our interpretation of past events as relevant to present and future conditions.

Our ability to relate the past and the future to each other -- i.e., to make sense of temporal change -- by means of an incremental sequentiality is the prime reason for studying the past and inserting it into the mechanisms describing the future. In management this is called <u>planning</u>. The notion of planning is, therefore, a temporal activity which is conceived for the sole purpose of selecting a desired sequence of states. Thus, our ability to plan is strictly a function of our ability to reconstruct the process of temporal change as a function of discretionary actions.

(2) Change

Change is a transformation process relating the past and the future. That is, if we could model the functional transformation of past into future

states, we would have determined the process of change. Change is in the
present, and it is here that management can influence future states. To
do so, a memory of past changes (i.e. memory of the past) is used to
estimate current states and forecasts of future changes, and to bring
about better decisions. To manage change, we must therefore, "manage the
view of the past", "manage the expectations of the future" and comprehend
how events are related to each other in time.

Psychologists have related time and change by noting that
perceptions of time estimates are inversely proportional to the number
of changes occurring in a given time interval. For example, given a
task requiring a large number of operations, subjects will estimate
the elapsed time to be shorter than if fewer operations were required.
Since this estimation is subjective, of course, different subjects will
make different estimates of elapsed time. Thus management may view the
time spent in performing a task as objective -- expressed in terms of
specific temporal milestones -- but workers may view it as subjective,
expressed as their perceptions of the task. If a worker considers a
task too long, this may mean that the task does indeed take a long time
or that the worker's estimation of time is long, implying impatience and
boredom with the task.

An understanding of time and change has technical as well as
behavioral implications for the modeling of management processes. In
such processes, two questions recur:

(1) Which "time steps" will characterize the evolution and recording of processes, and how will this be accomplished?[10] That is, what is the time interval used to operate on the system.

(2) What "planning horizon" is to be determined for the study of a specific process?

1. The first question is related to what is known as the "clock," that is, the "time step." It has to do with the mechanism for recording the flow of time. For example, if a system is observed and operated on at constant time intervals, then a question may arise concerning the length of the time interval. If the number of changes within the interval is large, a shorter interval may be necessary to record the temporal change. Operationally, however, a substantially long interval of time must be determined; otherwise, the computations required to reconstruct the process of temporal change may be too large. This problem is particularly acute, as we shall see in Chapter VI, in the simulation of time-related activities. It can be bypassed, however, if we recognize that the measurement of time is in effect a "temporal sampling" procedure. In studying a statistical population, we collect observations about it by sampling; similarly, we can assume that processes are "populations" which we investigate by collecting observations that are temporal samples of the process and can be used to infer its properties statistically. In this context, the number of observations and the procedure used in collecting these observations are of utmost importance in estimating properties of the processes.

Deciding how long the interval will be is by no means easy. The choice is determined by the following factors:

> The accuracy of temporal records
>
> The errors obtained by adopting a specific procedure for measuring time
>
> The costs incurred in selecting temporal observations

It is evident that if a significant number of changes occur in one time interval and if these changes are all lumped together as a single "observation," then there will be a substantial loss of information. This suggests a heuristic principle: The greater the number of changes in a time interval, the smaller the interval recording the flow of time.

2. The second question has to do with the "planning horizon". This is both technically important and conceptually significant. Typically, the planning time can be considered as one of the variables of a problem or it may be determined subjectively. Subjective determination is currently more common; it requires a certain understanding of processes and may be defined by five elements

(1) Effects of decision time

(2) Weight of memory

(3) Validity of the model over time

(4) Periodicity

(5) Tolerance of uncertainty and survival

First, we seek to determine the length of a planning horizon in terms of the time required to transform a decision into effects and side effects (see Figure I.3). For example, the planning-time horizon of a

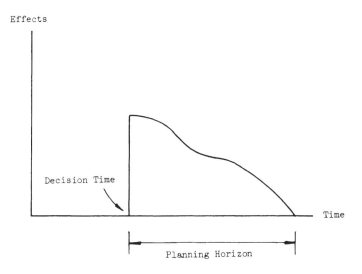

Figure 1.2: Decision Time Effects

machine is usually taken to be the effective life of that machine. Here, the initial investment in the machine, and the remaining operating and maintenance costs, are recuperated by the benefits that the machine yields. Since these benefits are obtained as long as the machine operates, planning the acquisition of machines can be based on the horizon described by their effective life. When this is unknown at the time of their acquisition, but is known to be a function of their utilization, repair, maintenance, and breakdowns, of new technology, and so on, we construct probabilistic estimates of the planning horizon (as shown in Figure 1.3).

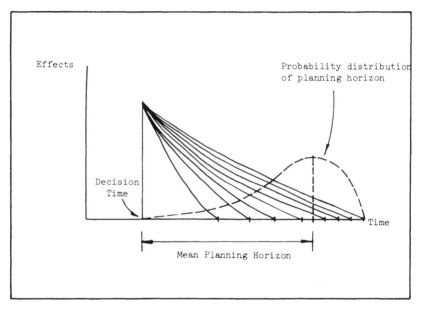

Figure 1.3: Probablistic Effects

In this case, the "decision-time" effects are probabilistic. When we are dealing with social problems, the effects of decisions in time are far more complicated than when we are dealing with machines. For example, suppose that an educational plan is being considered. To evaluate its desirability, its effects and side effects must be determined. But these may influence not only the future returns to, and satisfaction of, an individual but also his customs, his society, and possibly his descendants. How, then, does one determine a planning horizon? The multitude of factors involved preclude a planning horizon which could truly represent all the effects of a particular decision. For this reason, a certain amount of experience and foresight is required in determining the planning horizon.

The factor called "weight of memory" has to do with the effects of past states upon future states. The more that future states are dependent upon past history, the longer the planning horizon will be. In other words, if memory has a significant effect on future states and actions, in order to retrace these effects it is necessary to consider a very long planning horizon. The "weight of memory" of individuals similarly affects their planning horizon. Persons with poor memory tend to separate time into independent increments. Such persons, who are called myopic, do not evaluate the effects of current decisions upon future states. Instead, they consider the effects observed in the immediate future. Persons with good memory, on the contrary, do emphasize the interdependency of their actions in time and therefore can be said to use longer planning horizons (such persons are called nonmyopic.)

The third factor, validity of the model over time, makes reference to the increasing difficulties encountered in modeling future processes. If a process is technologically volatile -- that is, subject to sudden and unforseen changes and new developments -- then a fairly short planning horizon should be adopted. In general, when there is a good deal of uncertainty concerning future conditions and environmental variables, planning horizons ought to be short. For example, although the state of our world one or two generations hence is of importance to social and economic planners, forecasts based upon current conditions and knowledge are hardly reliable. Consequently, there must be continual reviews of the basic assumptions made in constructing a temporal model.

The fourth factor, the periodicity of the most important activities in a temporal process, may be used in the determination of the planning horizon. If a process reproduces itself every T periods, for practical purposes the planning horizon can be assumed to equal the length of one cycle of T periods. The period of a process as describing the planning horizon is, however, a problem of some complexity; we shall return to it in Chapter II.

The fifth and last factor -- tolerance of uncertainty and survival -- is used subjectively by both firms and individuals in selecting planning horizons. We note, for example, that firms in general tend to use smaller planning horizons, while governments, societies, and individuals tend to use longer planning horizons in evaluating the economic usefulness of certain projects. Why is there such a difference between these groups? In order to comprehend this, we must also note that they are different systems -- firms share may of the properties of machines, while societies and individuals share some properties of biological organisms. A firm's performance is usually evaluated in terms of one or a few standards of performance. To increase its efficiency, the firm has tended towards specialization of functions and, in the process, has developed a complex but fragile structure. This organizational structure, although workable in carrying out its original purposes and responsive to limited changes in the environment may have an unpredictable response in the face of great environmental changes. The firm is in fact limited by the range of available courses of action. Thus, it is usually in precarious equilibrium with its environment and may well be intolerant of unpredictable changes which could threaten its survival. Since the distant future is far more uncertain than the near future, firms will restrict planning horizons to levels which present tolerable uncertainty. Therefore, the firm's attitude toward uncertainty, its capacity to adapt and survive unpredictable changes will explain the choice of planning horizons.

Societies and individuals, on the other hand, share the capacity of biological systems to adapt to the environment, and will therefore be far more tolerant of the uncertainty of future outcomes. In other words, extremely great changes in the environment can be tolerated before the actual survival of the society or individual is threatened. The "lifelike" capacity to survive, expressed in adaptation to unforseen conditions, will thus allow much longer horizons than those adopted by firms. In summary, then, the capacity to survive and adaptation to the environment will increase the tolerance of uncertainty and hence the tolerance of longer planning horizons.

(3) Value

In operations management, time is often considered as a resource. This resource is _irreversible_, _limited_, _inelastic_, and _not storable_. Let us briefly examine each of these characteristics.

The irreversibility of time is, to some extent, a property used implicitly in determining _causal_ links explaining change. Following Russell,

> ...it is possible to obtain ostensive definitions of the words for temporal relations: 'preceding', 'succeeding', 'before', 'after', 'earlier', 'later'. When these words have come to be understood, we can understand such sentences as 'A precedes B' even when A and B are not part of one specious present, provided we know what is meant by 'A' and what is meant by 'B'.[11]

Time as a resource is also limited and inelastic. It cannot be stretched, it cannot be stopped, and it cannot be expanded as our needs prescribe.

Finally, since time cannot be stored, we must utilize it to the utmost as it becomes available. If an opportunity arises at a certain point in time and action is delayed, the opportunity may be lost forever. Other opportunities may recur, but never in the same form and rarely under the same conditions. Therefore, the pressures of time, or a lack of it, force us to <u>organize</u>, <u>allocate</u>, and <u>manage</u> time. In the <u>allocation of time</u>, we determine the sequence in which certain activities are performed; in the <u>management of time</u>, on the other hand, we seek to control temporal change. In other words, activities are planned, organized, and allocated so that what is intended should occur.

Because time has these characteristics, management must allocate it as other resources are allocated and make similar decisions concerning it. In practice, the timing of management decisions and their effects over time are essential factors in the success or failure of management. All too often, managers are found to have made a decision too early, too late, or at altogether the wrong time.

Although management is painfully conscious of time, managers usually find it difficult to consider the effects of a decision in time, for both organizational and psychological reasons. First, managers are faced with complex and sequential activities which are hard to trace, structure, and control. The complexity of temporal phenomena and the inability of managers to organize this complexity are prime reasons for the recurrent problem of management's inability to cope with time and change. A better structuring and modeling of activities that exist over time, based on the concepts of memory and change, may be of some help here. Second, there is the fact that people try to "fix" change in time.[12] That is, they are unable to focus on phenomena that vary over time; indeed, they seek methods which can blend the past and the future into a present. Such methods "immobilize" the flow of time, so that the present is the focus of the past and future. Figure 1.4 is a tentative attempt to show this.

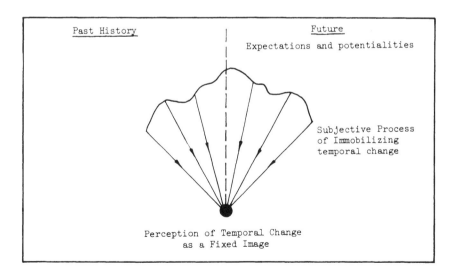

Figure 1.4: Immobilization of Temporal Change

When this sort of "fixing" is achieved, a static image is found by which we can grasp the implications and ramifications of change over time. The purpose of management in time is therefore to organize activities and "immobilize" the flow of time by expressing past, present, and future expectations and potentialities in terms of today. Once this is done, it can be said that a current operational choice is made as a result of the present image of all past and future states. We will next consider several examples of the notion of time and show how the notions and properties of time are of essential importance in management activities.

Examples

(1) Time and Memory

In modeling, memory is often used to trace causes in the past which have produced current effects. For example, the deterioration of a machine or piece of equipment is a function of the work load and usage it has been subjected to in the past. Similarly, reminiscing from the standpoint of today, we can understand that some current condition is the product of our past history, ideas, and social states.

(2) Past, Present, and Future

Planning is one of those activities which involve a simultaneous consideration of past, present, and future. For example, the past may be analyzed at some present instant of time to determine what relevance it has for forecasting the future. And forecasting is merely a present, but educated, guess about the future; past and future are combined to "estimate" states of change, and plans are then made on the basis of this estimate.

(3) Time, Operational and Real

Operational time may be defined in terms of those temporal milestones which have significance for modeling. For example, if the only changes are those occurring when some action is being contemplated, then operational time may be equated with the instants where action is being considered. Such actions may be contemplated continuously or discretely at regular intervals of time.

A striking example of the meaning of real time is found in the story of Captain James A. Mulligan, Jr., who in 1966 was captured by the North Vietnamese. In an interview after his release, Mulligan was able to recall the precise date of every significant event during his long captivity. For example, he knew the dates of various bombing raids, the dates when his colleagues had been captured, and the date of every change that took place in the routine or location of his prison life (The **New** York Times, April 1, 1973, p.1). Mulligan was aware of time and the record of time, but in terms of temporal milestones for which he had a memory.

Real time on the other hand, is defined as the objective unit which is used to register the flow of time. For example, seconds, hours, days, and years are objective units, milestones, used to indicate how much "real time" has elapsed. In systems science, the term "real-time" (hyphenated) is used to denote systems in which the response time is small enough to remain in close correspondence with real events.

(4) Time as a Resource

Expressions like "Make hay while the sun shines" and "Don't put off until tomorrow what you can do today" encourage prompt action and indicate

that time is a resource. The basic tenet of such maxims is that certain
propitious conditions are not necessarily recurrent. The exhortation to
do what one can while one can assumes that time is a resource which is
used up whether or not it is put to use.

I.3 Modeling Time Related Activities

Models are a simplified representation of some part of actual or
desired reality. Modeling, on the other hand, consists in determining
those elements that map this reality into a meaningful context which is
not overly complex. For this reason, modeling is not merely a technique
but an art blending the relevant aspects of reality with a descriptive yet
manageable and logical methodology. Modeling is a necessary activity when
the real processes at hand are complex ones. Time related activities are
such processes. To comprehend them and make sense of temporal change, it
is necessary that a modeling methodology be defined. The first part of
this chapter has outlined the essential elements required to model activities
occurring over time. These elements-memory, change, operational and
subjective time, past, present, future, etc. are ingredients required in
any modeling methodology which is to reproduce the process of change of
time related activities.

For example, we have stated in the preceding section that the notion
of memory is instrumental in relating the past to the present (as well as
the future to the present, in which case it is called expectation). In
order to model such a process, to obtain a quantitative measurement of
past and future, and to trace these measurements over time, it is
necessary to make simplifying assumptions about the process of temporal

change. Such assumptions are essential as they render manageable extremely complex and intractable processes. A model is, therefore, valid inasmuch as it is useful. The art of modeling time related activities consists then in finding what assumptions are most appropriate yielding insights about the process of change.

We now consider the essential problems faced when time is considered in the modeling process. Quantitative models will be considered in Chapter II. Here, specific attention is given to:

(1) The time structure of preferences
(2) The time structure of transformation processes
(3) The evolution of each process
(4) The temporal character of decisions, information, acquisition of information, and the coupling of decision and information systems.

1. The time structure of preferences is a particularly important and elusive subject.[13] It involves the determination of mechanisms scaling the desirability of certain outcomes over time and introduces some questions which are not easily resolved.

For example, the inter-relationship of current performance, decision, uncertainty, and future performance, are not clear. Questions regarding temporal comparability and tradeoffs of desired outcomes are often solved arbitrarily. Because of the importance of this problem, the structure of temporal preference will be given further attention in section I.4.

2. The "time structure of transformation processes" is the functional identity or the technology transforming a set of inputs into a set of outputs at a specific point of time. Four cases are possible:

    a. The transformation process does not change in time and is known with certainty.

    b. The transformation process changes in time and is known with certainty.

    c. The transformation process may (or may not) change in time and is probabilistically known.

    d. The transformation process is unknown.

The first and simplest case (case a) may describe, for example, a fixed-technology industry, an accounting or functional identity (see Figure I.5).

Figure I.5: An Accounting Structure - Input Output Model

Case b includes variable structure transformation processes. For example, a production process can be changed over time by a judicious use of new technology. Alternatively, a machine or piece of equipment can be used for one, two, or more production processes within a planning time. In this case, the transformation process is known; thus there is no uncertainty as to how a set of inputs is transformed into a set of outputs. However, the quality and quantity of outputs over time will be a function of the transformation process (see Figure I.6).

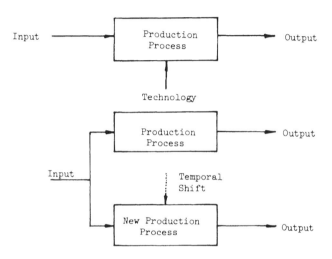

Figure I.6: Production Processes and Technology

Case c consists in determining a model of the transformation process which includes behavioral factors that can, at best, be represented by probabilistic phenomena. For example, the transformation of income into consumption is defined by an equation characterizing consumers' preferences, tastes, and 'propensities' to consume. Parameters of such a transformation may be estimated empirically, but this estimation implies that the true value of the parameter is unknown and our estimation of it is only probabilistic. If the transformation process does not change then, over time, it can be used repeatedly for planning. On the other hand, if the process does change, an adaptive mechanism reflecting changes over time must be included. These processes are represented in Figure 1.7.

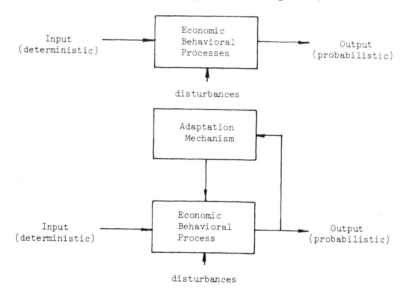

Figure 1.7: Economic Behavioral Processes

Case d, in which the transformation processes are unknown, is the one commonly encountered in social dynamics. For example, it may be postulated that the number of policemen in the street correlates with the crime rate. Exactly how we can translate one variable (policemen) into the other (crime), however, is simply not defined. Therefore, the problem of establishing the correlation requires that we devise mechanisms for identifying the transformation process and that we change our modeling of the process adaptively as experience and data are accumulated (see Figure I.8). It is evident that if the process also changes over time, we may then be in no position to evaluate past data for present estimation procedures.

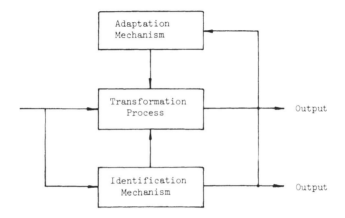

Figure I.8: Identification, Transformation and Adaptation

3. The evolution of processes is reflected in the time path of certain variables. In determining such a time path, there are numerical and descriptive difficulties. Numerical difficulties are encountered when complex and probabilistic systems of equations are integrated to show the evolution of a process over time. Descriptive difficulties are encountered when factors such as technical knowledge and innovation are essentially unknown and are to be reproduced and modeled as part of the processes. The question we then face pertains to the actual validity of a particular time path.

4. The temporal character and dependence of decisions and information on operational states necessitates certain mechanisms to record the

effects of decisions. When time is taken into account, the role of managers is in designing both management decision systems and information systems, tracing the history of the operational system, and using that history to forecast future states. This particular aspect of management over time is of considerable importance to operations analysis and will be investigated in Chapter IV.

To recapitulate, management of time and management over time consist in including temporal factors explicitly and on a real-time basis in the modeling of industrial and social systems. Making managers aware of the tools available for the analysis of processes will refine their understanding of time-related activities. This could be a first step in establishing management control over activities and change. Next we consider specific problems in management where time is an important factor. These problems will be developed further in Chapter II.

Examples: Temporal Problems

(1) Operational Processes

We can distinguish between two types of operational processes: those resulting in a product and those resulting in a service. Production processes are concerned with the control, monitoring, and operation of production resources, facilities, and equipment in order to produce something which can possibly be stored. Service processes, on the other hand, are concerned with producing something that cannot be stored. These processes are concerned with the determination of priorities and service configurations and with assignments of persons, machines, and priorities. Both production processes and service processes involve time and memory in an essential way. In a production process, inventory is an outcome of all past production decisions

and past demands for the product. Inventory is a "summary" of past history
and past effects and is therefore a memory mechanism. In service processes,
queues perform the same function as inventory, and they too are a summary
of all past demands and past services. The difference between production
and service processes, is that while in production processes the input to
the memory mechanism is controlled by management and the output is probabilistic and uncontrollable, in service processes the output is controlled
by management and the input is uncontrollable.

In production management, mechanisms based on past demands (another
memory mechanism) and marketing intelligence are used to generate demand
forecasts which in turn are used by managers. In service processes the
assumption is often made that two successive demands (i.e. arrivals into
the service system) are independent, and therefore an assumption of no
memory is made implicitly. Foremost among such "demand" processes is the
Poisson Process,[14] as we shall see in Chapter II. All these above processes
will be considered later in this book.

(2) Timing

The timing of certain actions in decision models is of utmost
importance. Managerial concern for timing is exemplified by these questions:

>When to produce a product
>
>When to order inventory lots
>
>When to expand the capacity of a productive process and
>how expansion would affect future financial, economic,
>or operational performance
>
>When to dispatch a vehicle on a route (a plane on a
>shuttle route, a train in a subway system, etc.)
>
>When to phase in or phase out a public program of
>construction

Many other such questions could be cited as examples. The time of capacity expansion is of particular importance, as it involves large present expenditures whose returns are probabilistic and will occur in the future. Moreover, committing a substantial part of a firm's resources to capacity expansion would tie up its flexibility if other opportunities occurred. Therefore, the *time* of expansion is a difficult managerial decision requiring careful analysis of all costs and benefits of making the expansion at a specific time.

(3) Time and Preference -- Discounting

Problems of time preference occur when questions are raised such as "Is consumption preferred now rather than later?" If the answer is yes, how is this preference expressed and ordered? For operational purposes, it is often necessary to find a basis for comparing the time values of two or more streams of consumption. One such basis is discounting. This consists in assuming that $S at time t is worth more than the same amount realized at a later time t+1. That is:

$$\text{Value } (\$S \text{ at time } t) > \text{Value } (\$S \text{ at time } t+1)$$

If two amounts of money obtained in two successive instants are to be comparable, it is necessary that some quantity Q be found such that:

$$\text{Value } (\$S \text{ at } t) = \text{Value } (\$Q \text{ at } t+1)$$

Assume that Q = S+R; then for the value of S and Q to be identical we require that:

$$S \text{ at } t = S+R \text{ at } t+1$$

where R is the quantity of money that we demand in order to forgo the consumption of S at t, and instead consume S+R at t+1. If we write

$R = rS$, we obtain: $Q = S+R = S+rS = S(1+r)$, where r is called the discount rate. If we repeat our computations from period $t+1$ to $t+2$, we find that:

$$S(1+r) \text{ at } t+1 = Q \text{ at } t+1 = Q(1+r) \text{ at } t+2 = S(1+r)^2 \text{ at } t+2$$

In general, for n periods after time t, we find that $S(1+r)^n$ is the amount of money we are willing to accept in order to forgo a consumption of S at t and instead consume $S(1+r)^n$ at time $t+n$. In this equation, r, the discount rate, expresses a temporal preference for money. Discounting, however, has several complications, which we shall see later (in Chapters II, V).

I.4 Decision Making and Decision Criteria

The establishment of quantitative and nonquantitative decision criteria in processes is a difficult problem. In particular, great difficulties are involved in specifying the time structure of these criteria (preferences). In practice, however, they are found to be necessary in distinguishing certain time paths, and are summarized below.

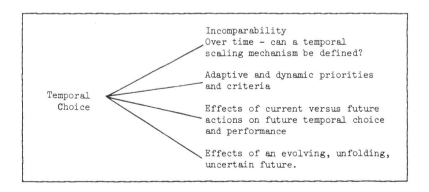

The purposes of this section are:

(1) To determine the characteristics of temporal criteria--
that is, criteria accounting for the time preference and

(2) To determine potential pitfalls in the selection of a
particular criterion.

The issues we face in establishing temporal criteria are connected with:

(1) Issues relating to the comparability or incomparability of current and future outcomes.

(2) The desire of managers to maintain a flexibility in decision making over time^{15} and to define the 'value' of flexibility.

(3) The effects of an uncertain and stochastic future upon time preference.

The nature of each of these will, to a great extent, determine the choice of temporal criteria.

(1) The comparability of current and future outcomes.

This comparability can be determined if we can formulate:

1. The evolution of "tastes"
2. The attitude toward postponement of choice, costs, and rewards

Operationally, changing tastes are reflected in:

Time-phasing of objectives

Elaboration of short-term and long-term goals, i.e., the definition of planning horizon

Adaptive mechanisms for the selection of objectives and priorities

In other words, the evolution of tastes renders most criteria of temporal choice invalid over long periods of time. For this reason, a frequent reevaluation of objectives in a process should be considered.

The attitude toward postponement of choice, costs, and rewards is to some extent determined by introducing discounting procedures. But the choice of procedures and of the discount rate, as we shall see, is not a simple task.

Discounting expresses the relative value of resources expressed in dollars. Typically, the value of future income is in relative terms, smaller than the same income realized now.

"A bird in the hand is worth two in the bush" -- this well-known adage, in a temporal context, means that what we have now is worth more than the same amount realized later. Discounting, however, is not without pitfalls. It may, for example, defer beyond any reasonable date the cost of current consumption. "Buy now, pay later" is a marketing philosophy and a psychological attitude regarding the selling of products and services, whereby the structure of temporal preferences is used to induce current consumption. A misuse of "discounting" can lead to situations where exhaustible resources are used now, with future generations paying the price of our greed. As the Bible says, "Fathers have eaten sour grapes, and the children's teeth are set on edge" (Jeremiah 31:29).

Therefore, discounting, although analytically attractive, is not a mechanism which may be applied without careful consideration of the short-term and long-term perspectives of the problem. Further research dealing with such problems is greatly needed; in Chapter II, we shall return to this important problem.

(2) The desire of managers to maintain flexibility in decision making over time and to express quantatively the value of such flexibility.

Over time, management values freedom of action and the development of opportunities. If future outcomes can be predicted with certainty, then there is indeed little reason to plan for flexibility. However, in practice, management is faced with an uncertain future and has to plan for possible contingencies. If programs are designed as an extrapolation of current reality, then they may not be able to withstand changing tastes, new political climates, expanding technological possibilities, or disasters. In other words, our inability to forecast structural and functional changes within a process makes it necessary to plan for unlikely and harmful disturbances to the system. Such situations lead to the establishment of systems whose objective over time is also to survive. This implies that management values the development of alternative actions which can meet unforseen and harmful effects. To do so, management incurs smaller risks in the pursuit of profits. Thus, there occurs a substitution of the need to survive for the need for larger profits obtained at greater risks. The greater the need to survive, the smaller the risks management will take. Moreover, attempts will be made by management to influence the outcomes of environmental disturbances as well, thereby reducing the risks of harmful disturbances. For example, many firms have substituted certain profit-maximization goals for goals of an increasing share of the market, or combined the two goals, thereby increasing their power to control market forces. Similarly, other firms have evolved and expanded by vertical integration. That is, they have internalized all the intermediate production processes from the supply of raw materials to the delivery of the finished product. (The Singer Corporation is a case in point). In the process of vertical integration, management is exercising an increasing influence on its environment -- except on the actual demand for its final product.

(3) The effects of an uncertain stochastic future upon time preference.

Stochastic processes over time will be fully discussed in Chapter II. However, there are several interesting issues having to do with the meaning and interdependence of three variables: time, preference, and risk and uncertainty[16] (see Figure I.9). Let us take these up now.

The deterministic criteria considered earlier had to do with ordering streams of returns in time and with establishing a scale for this order.

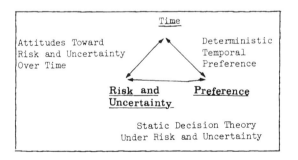

Figure I.9: Preference in Time and Risk and Uncertainty

In other words, the time of returns and the scale of returns were the only variables considered, and a functional form indicating the substitutability of these two variables expressed the temporal preference. Superimposing the element of risk and uncertainty on these two variables creates formidable problems. Now decision criteria no longer reflect a temporal preference only, but also an attitude toward risk and uncertainty concerning future states and outcomes.

The difficulties encountered in determining criteria which reflect both attitudes toward preference and risk over time necessitate certain a-priori assumptions about the behavior of decision makers. For example, consider a pessimistic decision maker preparing for the worst possible outcomes. His decision procedure is to estimate future outcomes and choose that decision strategy which will harm him least. Less pessimistic assumptions will, of course, result in different modes of reaching decisions. To allow the solution of temporal problems under risk and uncertainty, decision criteria are expressed in a deterministic form as a function of time and as a function of the parameters of the probability distribution characterizing knowledge of the processes over time. If the uncertainty of the processes and parameters becomes too large, decision makers devise systems which can reduce it. These systems, called information systems, normally emphasize the reduction of uncertainty with respect to the near future rather than the distant future.[17]

The propensity of decision makers to reduce uncertainty in time gives rise to a variety of activities: inquiring, estimating, learning, and forecasting. Inquiring is concerned with the processes involved in seeking relevant information. Estimating transforms this information into a form which may be used by decision makers. Learning consists in determining mechanisms which can incorporate sequentially the results of inquiry into the estimation processes. Finally, forecasting is the process of inferring the future. Each of these activities applies to both processes and criteria. Therefore, the costs of conducting such activities also reflect the attitudes of decision makers toward risk and uncertainty over time.

Problems concerning attitudes toward risk over time have attracted much attention in the context of investment decisions under uncertainty.[18] In essence, investments are present expenditures incurred to obtain future returns. Under uncertainty, such returns are stochastic. Thus investment is determined by the excess of net returns over investment outlays, once these amounts are made consistent with the attitudes toward preference and risk over time. Since it is difficult to solve problems where both time and risk are specific dimensions, finance managers utilize operational methods which incorporate the effects of time and risk on the choice of investment projects. These are:[19]

(1) The discount-rate mechanism -- taken to reflect both time preference and risk.

(2) Certainty equivalents, which consist in the selection of a utility function that remains static over time.

The discount-rate mechanism in adjusting for both time preference and risk is of particular importance in applications of financial management and will be considered later on. Certainty equivalents, more commonly used in management, will be discussed here.

The process of replacing a set of possible outcomes by a single one is called a <u>certainty equivalent</u> (see Figure I.10). In optimizing a system

Figure I.10: The Observation of Uncertainty with Certainty Equivalents

under uncertainty (i.e., solving for its best properties), there is no operational meaning for "probability." In fact, probabilities are merely weights which <u>represent</u> what we believe is uncertainty. Although we call these weights "probabilistic," they are deterministic representations of the system. The quantitative methods and tools we apply are also of an essentially deterministic nature. This point is extremely important and emphasizes the need for, and usefulness of, certainty equivalent methods. Thus, the certainty equivalent is a necessary tool which can replace what is mathematically, computationally, and operationally an intractable system by an "equivalent" tractable representation of that system. The methods for determining certainty equivalents are often called separation,[20] deterministic equivalents,[21] and certainty equivalence.[22] All perform the same function and these will be considered in Chapter V.

It is evident from the foregoing discussion that the choice of temporal preference functions is not a simple matter. Such functions cannot be determined by mere extension of static preference functions. In static choice situations -- situations where choice is based on the outcomes of one period -- we typically order all possible outcomes and choose the one with the greatest benefits. A direct extension of this approach over time would be to <u>separate</u> the choice of each time period and select a choice for each of these periods. Thus, temporal choice in this context is "timeless" and does not reflect the value of events as they occur over time. Also, the coupling of time and memory, reflected in this case by the substitutability of temporal choice, is not accounted for in dynamic versions of static preference functions. Thus, preferences over time have both intrinsic and extrinsic characteristics which may not always be easily determined in a quantitative way. Nonetheless, a quantification of the structure of temporal preference is required if tools of analysis are to be applied in selecting decision strategies and in designing systems. Such quantitative criteria should[23]

(1) Be well defined with respect to time

(2) Reflect managerial responsibilities

(3) Be expressed as a function of variables which may be influenced directly, indirectly, or both by time

(4) Reflect the essential dimensions of the system

(5) Be analytically and functionally tractable, leading to simple numerical results

(6) Provide, after appropriate analysis, insights and decision rules for the management of the system over time

Although not all quantitative criteria can satisfy all these requirements, choice of criteria can be based on how close they come to satisfying each condition.

I.5 Time and Operational Models

Prior to concluding this chapter we shall provide examples and activities in operational modeling which involve time. These examples, for the most part, will be pursued further in later chapters. Here, we merely point out how time becomes an essential factor in modeling operational processes. In Chapter II, additional examples are included.

(1) Planning

"We like to think that the highest rewards go to those who plan and that attention to the future brings benefits even in the small events of everyday life. In our society, because of its structure and values, planning is a compulsive activity; we take for granted that it is good to plan. But we are not clear as to what good planning is. Does good planning mean that the future is accurately predicted and adequately prepared for? Or does it mean that an intended future state is brought to pass?"[24]

Such questions epitomize the confusion surrounding the nature and functions of planning activities, and the question of whether these activities are tied to the policy-making process.[25] This section will describe the functions of planning resulting from the interactions of time and risk as discussed earlier.

In a perspective of time, planning includes two essential activities

Organization of events in time

Reduction of uncertainty in time

Organization is a basic human activity which consists in transforming a set of seemingly unrelated events into a coherent whole. Over time, this problem is complicated, because it requires a very clear understanding of the causes of change. That is, in temporally organizing[26] a set of events, activities, and actions, we seek to establish not only their causal links but how these links are maintained over time.

The second activity--reduction of uncertainty in time--is the attempt to replace a set of strings of unknown events in time by one or more strings of presumed events. In planning, we face an unmanageable number, indeed an unlimited number, of possible futures. Therefore, if we are to make a reproduction of the future in the present, we must determine a substitute for it. This substitute is not what will necessarily occur; it is our guess about what may occur.

The process of inferring and "imagining" the future and the mechanics of this process are of extreme importance. One example of such planning activities is the Delphi technique,[27] by which a forecast of the future is established by means of a set of independent educated guesses about that future, usually made by experts. Each expert is considered a "statistical sample" describing certain outcomes in the future. Experts are chosen so that the "samples" will be informative, i.e., better predictors of the future. The same technique could be applied without experts, of course; we could predict the state of technology in the next century by a random sampling of persons passing in Times Square. The problem, however, is to obtain an acceptable prediction of the future; to do this, the "samples" we collect must be credible.

Whenever a set of events has been temporally organized and a reduction of uncertainty has been achieved, a model of the future has in fact been constructed. It is at this point that alternative courses of action can be tested for their future impact. By manipulating the model on the basis of credible assumptions concerning the future, we obtain credible time paths of the variables with which we are most directly concerned. Planning may then be defined as an activity in time designed to attain a set of desired states using a series of actions and strategies. It would be concerned with the following:

> The elaboration of goals (expressed as desired states) and their realization in time
>
> The elaboration of available means over time (i.e., possible courses of action)
>
> The organization and allocation in time of the available means necessary to achieve the desired goals

Planning in this sense will be the core of the rest of the book. In Chapter III, we will be concerned with defining and elaborating planning problems whose purpose is to chart a course of action in time. Examples and applications to business and socio-economic areas are also considered. Finally, in Chapters IV, V, and VI, the quantative description and manipulation of such planning problems will be outlined.

The future is not entirely a function of our actions or strategies. Our model of the future is also subject to environmental inputs and disturbances which are usually unknown and uncontrollable. Thus, while we are free to take whatever actions we may choose, we cannot specify future events beforehand. To make the relevant choices more manageable, and to gain more information concerning the impact of an action upon a future, we resort to what will be called here information planning. For example, when a manufacturer investigates the potential demand for something he plans to produce, he is essentially "information planning". That is, by gathering information and estimating processing costs, he achieves more relevant and credible knowledge of his environment and thus increases the manageability of his firm. This "environment" in this case is the existence of similar products on the market, the strength of the competition, and the needs and demands of consumers. Given an assessment of potential successes and pitfalls in production, the manufacturer can face the future with

greater confidence and justified expectations. In this process, the
manufacturer has not specified the future, but he has identified it in
terms of a probable succession of events which he is willing to accept in
designing a course of action. The processes of information planning and
planning a course of action are summarized in Figure I.11. Such problems
will be of essential concern in Chapter V, where methods for designing
information-planning strategies are outlined.

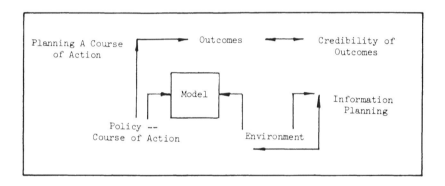

Figure I.11: Planning a Course of Action

(2) Planning the Acquisition and Replacement of Machines

The problem as seen by businessmen is to maximize the value of
machines and other equipment used in the operation of businesses. Planning
the acquisition of a new machine, a machine's maintenance program, or the
replacement of a machine by another newer machine involves complex analyses
and considerable uncertainty about the future. This uncertainty concerns
the effective life of the machine (that is, the period during which it is
used), new technological developments which make the machine obsolete,

possible breakdowns and failures. These are factors which make the economic evaluation of a machine extremely difficult. In this example, we shall consider the essential elements which render a machine "productively" and "technically" obsolete. Below (in Chapter II), specific planning models will be constructed and resolved.

In general, most pieces of equipment tend to become productively less efficient as their age increases, until they reach a point at which it is no longer deemed profitable to use them. In such cases, we say that the machine is productively obsolete. There are two opposing factors: the aging process reflecting physical wear and tear and utilization and maintenance programs ensuring smooth and efficient operation of the machine.

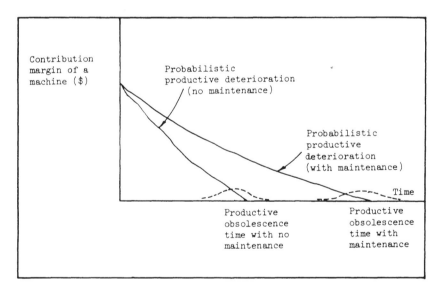

Figure I.12: Machine Productive Obsolescence

Here, management can influence the rate at which a machine becomes productively obsolete by planning an appropriate maintenance program. A machine may, however, become obsolete before it reaches a state of productive obsolescence. Obsolescence is then expressed in the appearance of newer machines on the market which have greater productivity. When a machine is worth replacing by another one, we say the machine is technically obsolete. That is, while productive obsolescence alludes to a machine's inability to perform certain functions economically, technical obsolescence reflects the availability of alternative and more economical machines. (see Figure I.13).

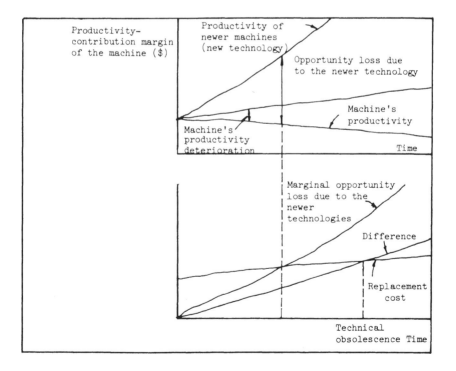

Figure I.13: Machine's Technical Obsolescence

Businessmen's calculations to retire machines are not only based on the ability of the machine to contribute to profits, but also on the competitive value (the opportunity costs) of new and future machines. Thus, the decision to replace a machine is also based on the opportunity costs of not buying the machines.

To demonstrate this point further, consider the dilemma faced by the airline industry. It is commonly acknowledged that airlines have to pay for bigger and faster planes before the older generation planes "have paid for themselves." In our terms, it can be argued that the new planes will generate a stream of income which will also cover the cost of the older planes. Such an income stream may be derived by an increased productive capacity, easier maintenance, or cheaper operational costs. In this case, the question faced by airline managers is not whether to buy the new planes, but when to retire the older planes and introduce the new ones. Thus, planes assigned to passenger transportation may, after the appearance of new planes, be assigned to freight transportation. Although the plane is deemed productively efficient in freight transportation, it has become obsolete for passenger transportation.

A simultaneous consideration of machine production and technical obsolescence leads to a variety of interesting planning problems. These would involve determination of: (1) the future benefits derived by use of the machine; (2) the maintenance costs and costs of repairs; (3) the aging processes of machines describing both productive deterioration and evolution of the probability of machine failure; (4) opportunity costs of not using newer machines appearing on the market; (5) opportunity costs of not using the machines in other production processes. More specifically, the following planning problems could be considered:

1. Given a probabilistic life of a machine and given its future (and present) stream of costs and returns, should the machine be acquired?

2. Given the cost of a machine, its maintenance and effectiveness and deterioration functions, and given the evolution in time of its salvage value, what is the best maintenance program?

3. When a machine becomes productively obsolete, what is the best alternative productive process?

4. Given two machines with two essentially identical functions but different operational characteristics, when is it worth replacing one machine by another?

In Chapter II, such problems will be described quantitatively and will be solved in Chapters IV and V.

(3) Buy Now Pay Later

The motto, "buy now pay later," and its British equivalent, "the never never," indicate that individuals finance current consumption by trading larger amounts of future income for it. The premiums paid to induce creditors to forego present income to finance the current consumption of debtors is called interest when the debt is classed as the loan of money, or the broader term finance charge is used to cover both the loan of money and the financing of goods. Irving Fisher [28] perceptively pointed out that the interest premium paid to finance current consumption really represented the efforts of individuals to alter the size and time shapes of their expected future real incomes in order to first, satisfy their impatience for current consumption and second, make the most of their opportunities to invest.[29]

Fisher indicated the importance of a consumer's time preference, or impatience in choosing the rate at which he was willing to discount future income to obtain additional present consumption. His analysis has been extended by Hirshleifer[30] and, Juster and Shay[31], to apply the theory of time preference to consumers' investment decisions. These analyses stress the importance of the individual's subjective borrowing costs. These costs are determined by the individual's rate of time preference or discount rate, in relation to the market rate at which they can borrow to achieve the gains or consumer's surplus. This consumer's surplus is implicit in the decision to purchase a consumer durable good. Yet no one has estimated, or ever attempted to estimate to our knowledge, the actual discount rate used by consumers in making their investment decisions.[32] The empirical estimation of differences in consumers' discount rates and the relation of these rates to market rates is the aim of this application. Specifically, in the sections of this book which follow, we shall attempt to determine the probability distribution of the consumer's discount rate and use that distribution to estimate the discount rate of borrowers, and the consumers' surplus derived from the use of credit.

I.6 Summary

The purpose of this chapter has been to outline those elements, particular to processes, which ought to be considered in the modeling of operational systems over time. Time and the coupling of time and operations analysis have been investigated. Essentially, a system was outlined for elaborating plans and designing models in a temporal framework. The inclusion of time in the modeling and analysis of operational systems is by no means easy, but it is a factor that must be considered in the practice of operations management. Making management aware of time and processes is a step toward the development of real-time managerial technologies. The first step, however, is to understand the ramifications and implications of time and change in operations management. This chapter has elaborated on those temporal dimensions relevant to operations management. Specific attention was given to the meaning of time and the quantification of temporal systems (the latter aspect of this issue will become more central in Chapter II). The essential elements of the chapter were:

        (1) Inclusion of time in operations management problems

        (2) Transfer problems in switching from static to dynamic modes of analysis

        (3) Problems of time preference

        (4) Objective and subjective time in operations management

        (5) Problems found in selecting decision criteria for processes

These elements form a foundation upon which a quantitative theory of planning can be established. Chapter III, IV and V will deal with those dimensions of the problem.

FOOTNOTES

1. In static conditions, the effects of decisions in time cannot be traced. In dynamic conditions, however, these effects are explicitly given in terms of the time of occurrence of the decision and the cumulative effects of change over time.

2. Time has always been subjected to scrutiny and analysis. It is therefore impossible to give even a representative sample of the literature on time. Recently, psychologists such as Fraisse (8), Piaget (20), Wallis (30), Doob (5) have dealt with the concept and perception of time. An extensive bibliography to that effect can be found in Doob. Philosophers, such as Russell (21) and Bergson (3), have also faced the implications of time, and have defined time more objectively than, say, psychologists. Other references on time, not referred to in the text, are given at the end of this chapter as additional references.

3. See Frederick Taylor (28).

4. Piaget's experiments (20) were concerned with the measurement of perceptions of time in children. He found, much as Pavlov did with dogs, that babies had a sensory perception of time. Therefore, for them, the notion of time is subjective, associated with the occurrence of specific events.

5. To avoid confusion, the usefulness of memory as a concept is realized when quantitative descriptions of processes can be obtained which retrace the occurrence of past states backwards from the present time. The memory of individual persons is far more complex as the processes tracing past events are influenced by learning and forgetting mechanisms.

6. In other words, the effect of time and temporal change can be quantitatively recorded only through mechanisms which carry the effects of past decisions and states over time. A temporal independence is equivalent to a "timeless" situation in which decisions made at one point in time are independent of past and future states.

7. Saint Augustine (1), Book XI, **xx**.

8. In operational management this analogy is most important. Since decisions are always made in the <u>present</u>, "future" decisions are merely planned or forecasted decisions based on our present perception and analysis of past and future forecasted data.

9. See Wallis (30) for an excellent discussion of this problem.

10. In other words, what time units are to be adopted: days, weeks, months, years, hours, minutes, seconds?

11. See Russell (21), p. 210-217.

12. This point is stressed by Bergson (3).

13. Koopmans (13, 14, 15) and Beckmann (2), as well as many other authors, have been interested in the implications of decision making and preference over time.

14. The Poisson process, is a probabilistic process which makes the following assumptions: (i) the probability of events occurring in time are independent; (ii) the mean number of occurrences per unit time is a constant. The Poisson process is useful as it is both a plausible and analytically attractive process.

15. By flexibility, we mean a number of alternative courses of action that can be taken by management which will lead to different results. The number of choices open to management when certain conditions arise is therefore a measure of flexibility. A problem associated with flexibility in decision making is the contingency planning problem -- consisting in the planning for a set of possible futures, given that only one will occur. This problem, of extremely practical importance, has been studied by Starr (26).

16. An extremely clear and simple discussion of decision making and uncertainty can be found in Miller and Starr (19).

17. This observation is similar to the use of discounting mechanisms in time preference. In other words, since we value more outcomes in the near future rather than the distant future, we would also prefer smaller risks associated to these outcomes. To obtain a comparability in time between risks of outcomes, we use methods called risk-adjusted discounting rates (see Hirschleifer (11)).

18. Just as we have an attitude towards a stream of income in time -- reflecting our time preference -- we can also have an attitude towards risk -- reflecting a "value" of the risks associated to a particular stream. Problems of attitudes towards risky time streams are extremely complicated and do not have, as yet, a completely satisfactory solution.

19. This problem, of primary importance in finance, has attracted much attention; several solutions based on utility analysis of uncertain future streams of income have been suggested (see Hirschleifer (11), Markowitz (18)).

20. There is much confusion in the literature concerning certainty equivalent methods. Our meaning here for separation, deterministic equivalents, and certainty equivalence will be specified. For a more complete study of separation, see Simon (24), Theil (29) and the more general paper of Wonham (32).

21. Deterministic equivalents are based on approximations to which we apply the methods of separation. See Sage and Melsa (22).

22. Certainty equivalence -- commonly used in finance -- refers to the replacement of the expected utility of a stream of returns by the utility of the expected returns. In other words, we replace a set of random variables by the estimates of those variables.

23. These criteria are adapted from Groff and Muth (9) for time-dependent systems.

24. Starr (25).

25. See, for example, Le Breton and Henning (16); Starr (25), Bright (4); Warren (31).

26. That is, finding the order in which a set of activities occurs or ought to occur, and the duration of each activity.

27. See Helmer (10). The Delphi technique was developed at Rand by Helmer and T. J. Gordon.

28. See Tapiero and Shay (27).

29. See Fisher's (7) early and outstanding treatise.

30. There have been attempts to ascertain the rates of return which accrue to customers from the credit purchase of consumer durables at market rates of charge of credit. See for example Dunkelberg and Stephenson (6).

REFERENCES

(1) Augustine (of Hippo), Saint. *Confessions*. Translated by Dr. E.B. Pusey. New York, E.P. Dutton and Company, 1950.

(2) Beckmann, M.J., "Decisions over Time," in C.B. McGuire and R. Radner (Eds.). *Decision and Organization*. New York, North-Holland/American Elsevier, 1972, pp. 141-161.

(3) Bergson, H. *Durée et Simultaneité*. Paris, Alcan, 1922.

(4) Bright, J. (Ed.). *Technological Planning*. Cambridge, Mass., Harvard University Press, 1962.

(5) Doob, L.W. *Patterning of Time*. New Haven, Conn., Yale University Press, 1971.

(6) Dunkelberg, W.C. and J. Stephenson, "Rates of Return and Consumer Durables," *Journal of Finance*, December 1964.

(7) Fisher, I. *The Theory of Interest: As Determined by Impatience to Spend Income and Opportunity to Invest It*. New York, Macmillan Company, 1930; New York, Kelley & Millman Inc., 1954.

(8) Fraisse, P. *Psychologie du Temps*. Paris, Presses Universitaires, 1957.

(9) Groff, G.K. and J.F. Muth. *Operations Management; Analysis for Decisions*. Homewood, Illinois, Irwin, 1972.

(10) Helmer, O. *Social Technology*. New York, Basic Books, 1966.

(11) Hirschleifer, J. *Investment, Interest and Capital*. Englewood Cliffs, New Jersey, Prentice Hall, 1970.

(12) Juster, T.F. and R.P. Shay, "Consumer Sensitivity to Finance Rates: An Empirical and Analytical Investigation," Occasional Paper 88, *National Bureau of Economic Research*, 1964.

(13) Koopmans, T.C., "On Flexibility of Future Preference," in M.W. Shelly II and G.L. Bryan (Eds.). *Human Judgements and Optimality*. New York, Wiley and Sons, 1964, pp.

(14) —————————, "Representation of Preference Orderings Over Time," in C.B. McGuire and R. Radner (Eds.). *Decision and Organization*. New York, North-Holland/American Elsevier, 1972, pp. 79-101.

(15) ──────────, "Utility Analysis of Decisions Affecting Future Well-Being," Econometrica, April 1950, pp. 175-176.

(16) Le Breton, P.P. and D.A. Henning. Planning Theory. Englewood Cliffs, New Jersey, Prentice Hall, 1961.

(17) McGuire, C.B. and R. Radner (Eds.). Decision and Organization. Vol. 12 in the series: STUDIES IN MATHEMATICAL AND MANAGERIAL ECONOMICS, Ed. H. Theil. New York, North-Holland/American Elsevier, 1972.

(18) Markowitz, H.M. Portfolio Selection. New York, Wiley and Sons, 1959.

(19) Miller, D. and M.K. Starr. The Structure of Human Decisions. Englewood Cliffs, New Jersey, Prentice Hall, 1967.

(20) Piaget, J. Le Developpement de la Notion du Temps Chez L'Enfant. Paris, Presses Universitaires de France, 1946.

(21) Russell, B. Human Knowledge: Its Scope and Limits. New York, Simon and Schuster, 1948.

(22) Sage, A. and J.L. Melsa. Estimation Theory with Applications to Communications and Control. New York, McGraw Hill Book Company, 1971.

(23) Shackle, G.L.S. Time in Economics. Amsterdam, North-Holland, 1958.

(24) Simon, H.A., "Dynamic Programming under Uncertainty with a Quadratic Criterion Function," Econometrica, 24, 1956, pp. 74-81.

(25) Starr, M.K. Management: A Modern Approach. New York, Harcourt, Brace, Jovanovich, 1971.

(26) ──────────, "A Quantitative Approach to Management Planning: Contingency Planning Models," presented at the IESE Conference in Barcelona, Spain, in June 1970. Published in Proceedings, 1971.

(27) Tapiero, C.S. and R.P. Shay, "Buy Now-Pay Later, Consumers' Discount Rates and Consumers' Surplus," Columbia University, Research Paper, 1974.

(28) Taylor, F.W. The Principles and Methods of Scientific Management. New York, Harper and Row, 1911.

(29) Theil, H. Optimal Decision Rules for Government and Industry. Amsterdam, North-Holland, 1964.

(30) Wallis, R. Time: Fourth Dimension of the Mind. New York, Harcourt, Brace, Jovanovich, 1966.

(31) Warren, E.K. Long-Range Planning. Englewood Cliffs, New Jersey, Prentice Hall, 1966.

(32) Wonham, W.M., "On the Separation Theorem of Stochastic Control," SIAM Journal on Control, 6, 1968, pp. 312-326.

Additional References

Baumol, W.J. Economic Dynamics. 2nd ed. New York, Macmillan, 1959.

Bergson, H. Creative Evolution. Modern Library Edition. New York, Random House, 1944.

——————. Time and Free Will. New York, Humanities' Press, 1959.

Bolton, L. Time Measurement. Princeton, New Jersey, Van Nostrand, 1924.

Churchman, C.W. Prediction and Optimal Decision. Englewood Cliffs, New Jersey, Prentice Hall, 1961.

Davis, R., "Time Uncertainty and the Estimation of Time-Intervals," Nature, 195, 1962, pp. 311-312.

De Grazia, S. Of Time, Work and Leisure. New York, Twentieth Century Fund, 1962.

Fraisse, P., "Time: Psychological Aspects," in D.L. Sills (Ed.) International Encyclopedia of the Social Sciences, Vol. 16. New York, Macmillan & The Free Press, 1968, pp. 25-30.

Fraser, J. (Ed.). The Voices of Time. New York, George-Braziller, 1966.

Gale, R.M. (Ed.). The Philosophy of Time. Garden City, New York, Doubleday Anchor Books, 1967.

Goody, J., "Time: Social Organization," in D.L. Sills (Ed.). International Encyclopedia of the Social Sciences, Vol. 16. New York, Macmillan & The Free Press, 1968, pp. 30-42.

Hart, A.G. Anticipation, Uncertainty and Dynamic Planning. Chicago, University of Chicago Press, 1940.

Heidegger, M. The Phenomenology of Internal Time-Consciousness. Translated by J. Churchill. The Hague, Martinus Nijhoff, 1964.

Huxley, A. Doors of Perception. New York, Harper and Row, 1954.

Janet, P. L'Evolution de la Memoire et la Notion du Temps. Paris, Chahin, 1928.

Moore, W.E. Man, Time and Society. New York, Wiley and Sons, 1963.

Pieron, H., "Les Problemes Psychologiques de la Perception du Temps," Année Psychologique, 24, 1923, pp. 1-25.

Sartre, J-P. Being and Nothingness. New York, Citadel Press, 1965.

Toffler, A. Future Shock. New York, Bantam Books, 1971.

Toulmin, S. and J. Goodfield. The Discovery of Time. New York, Harper and Row, 1965.

Wallace, M., "Temporal Experience," Psychology Bulletin, 51, 1960. pp. 213-237.

Whitehead, A.N. Process and Reality. New York, Social Science Publishers, 1929.

Whitrow, G.I. The Natural Philosophy of Time. New York, Harper Torchbooks, 1963.

Wiener, N. The Human Use of Human Beings. Boston, Houghton-Mifflin, 1950.

Yaker, H., Osmond, H. and F. Cheek (Eds.). The Future of Time; Man's Temporal Environment. Garden City, New York, Doubleday Anchor Books, 1972.

Problems

1. Alvin Toffler, in his book, <u>Future Shock</u>, describes the present as an "intrapolation" of the future. In other words, Toffler claims that the present is conditioned by our view of the future. How is this different from our understanding of and analysis of historical processes in comprehending the present?

2. Explain the motives of persons to save. How are these motives related to the persons' expectations of the future?

3. Contrast two producers -- one choosing an elaborate forecasting mechanism to estimate the demand for his product, the other choosing less elaborate forecasting mechanisms. If both obtain the same expected forecasts, in what ways does the more elaborate forecasting mechanism reduce uncertainty concerning the future.

4. Buying an expensive piece of equipment such as an advanced technology aircraft, a computer, etc., involves a commitment to a future technological stability. Explain then the role of future uncertainty concerning technological developments in influencing the decision to buy a new piece of equipment today.

5. Investment decisions implicitly (and sometimes explicitly) account for time, timing, temporal preference, temporal risk. Discuss how this is achieved?

6. You are promised and accept an amount of $\$x_1$ a year from now instead of $\$x_0$ today.
    (i) How does the difference $\$(x_1 - x_0)$ represent your time preference?
    (ii) What is the discount rate?
    (iii) If $u(x,t)$ is an amount worth $\$x$ t years from now, what properties would you associate to the function $u(x,t)$? Give some examples (graphical and non-graphical) for the potential form $u(x,t)$.
    (iv) If y is defined as the risk of obtaining $\$x$ t years from now, and $u(x,y,t)$ is worth $\$x_0$ today, how would x_0 change if x, y and t increase? decrease?
    (v) Can you adjust for the time value of money? Can you adjust for the effects of risk over time? Discuss and compare discounting and risk-adjusted methods.

7. A time preference scale can be found by comparing your <u>indifference</u> for two outcomes occurring in time. Similarly, <u>impatience</u> for future outcomes can be used to determine a scale for temporal preference. How do indifference and impatience differ?

8. Discounting for time is an opportunity cost. Explain.

9. Describe the effects of inflation on a decision to buy a car on credit. What is the role of your expectations in terms of your future income, expected benefits derived from the car and the expected cost of the car?

10. In 1972 the El-Paso Gas Company signed a contract with the Algerian Government for the delivery of gas for the next twenty years. Can you justify the economic rationale of such a decision in terms of **a. Expectations of future world market conditions.** b. Uncertainties concerning future energy supplies. Would you consider that signing this contract would reduce future uncertainty faced by the El-Paso Gas Company?

11. Explain why the cost of signing a contract is implicit in the certainty equivalent models we derive of the future.

12. Explain how "buy now-pay later" induces current consumption at future expense. What is the role of your temporal preference in acquiring a car on credit terms?

13. Contrast and compare the productive and the economic life of a machine.

14. Contrast and compare the use of data and experience in assigning probabilities to the occurrence of certain events.

15. Discuss the differences and similarities between; forecasting, prediction, extrapolation, expectation, and intrapolation.

Chapter II: Planning and Models - Over Time

Chapter I established the essential properties of time which make it uniquely important to the management process. Application of these concepts and properties of time to management problems requires, however, that models and functions of planning be further refined and that the tools necessary to reproduce the process of change be defined. The purpose of this chapter is to define more precisely planning models, and provide a quantitative formulation of memory processes. We shall also consider several planning examples which will be developed further and resolved in Chapters III, IV and V.

In section II.1, a classification of planning activities according to the planning horizon and the nature of uncertainty is indicated. Such a characterization of planning problems will be helpful in defining the problems of control in Chapter III. In section II.2, the meaningfulness of difference and differential equations for example, to the quantification of memory processes is sought.

For the solution of differential equations, we refer to appendix II.1 at the end of this chapter; and for specific applications we refer to section II.3. In section II.4, memory described by stochastic processes is considered specifically by Markov, Wiener-Levy, Poisson and other processes as well as stochastic integrals and stochastic differential equations are defined. Section II.5 provides examples to such processes. While the examples in section II.3 provide a basis for problems of control solved in Chapter IV, the examples in section II.5 provide a basis for the stochastic control problems solved in Chapter V.

Finally, in section II.6, discount rates and discounting are re-examined by considering discounting as a stochastic process. This chapter therefore provides a foundation for the quantitative formulation of dynamic models.

II.1 A Classification of Planning Activities

It is convenient to classify planning activities according to the planning horizon and the "uncertainty" of the environment. These two factors will prescribe what tools and approaches are to be used in developing plans.

The planning horizon forms the basis of three types of planning activities;

>Incremental Planning
>Long term Planning
>Intermediate Planning

Incremental planning emphasizes a short planning horizon, adjusts adaptively to a changing environment, does not involve much uncertainty, is very flexible, and emphasizes short-term performance.[1] Production planning is one example of incremental planning. It prescribes production decisions for a relatively small planning time, as a function of past history and of anticipated demands within this relatively short time.

Long-term planning considers long planning horizons, and therefore involves large uncertainties. It typically involves decisions whose effects will be felt over long periods of time. Adjustments to a changing environment are not easy; long-term planning emphasizes stable operating conditions and performance. Examples of long-term planning are educational planning, capacity expansion of a firm, and aggregate economic planning. In each of these activities, present actions are taken and costs are incurred whose effects and benefits will be felt over long periods of time.

Intermediate planning involves a combination of incremental and long-term planning. It consists in establishing a sequence of shorter-range plans which will be implemented in the future. Thus intermediate planning emphasizes both short and long horizons. It maintains temporal flexibility, reduces the risks of current long-term decisions, and emphasizes both performance and stability.[2] An example of intermediate planning is the sequential implementation of a multiple-facility capacity-expansion program. Here, the uncertainty of incurring a single capacity expansion at one point in time is reduced by implementing smaller capacities over a long period of time. Although the expansion costs may be larger, benefits are realized by reducing the uncertainty of decisions and by maintaining flexibility over time.[3]

The uncertainty of the environment gives rise to four planning situations: (i) Planning under certainty -- that is, in a perfectly predictable environment, (ii) Planning under uncertainty but with a stochastically known and partially controlled environment, (iii) Planning under uncertainty but with a stochastically known and uncontrolled environment, (iv) Planning under complete uncertainty -- that is, in a completely random environment.

The various planning situations differ in approach, emphasis, method of analysis, and interpretation of results. The degree of uncertainty concerning the environment and the future is actually the essential factor in differentiating planning problems. The planning horizon is a special case in point, since we assume that the longer the planning time, the greater the uncertainty. Thus, a planning activity is conceived entirely as a function of our ability to make a dependable model of the process of change. When the environment and the future are perfectly predictable, we say that we are planning under certainty. This and other planning situations are discussed next.

In the control problems to be outlined, we will allude to disturbances, control variables and state variables. Disturbances are known or probabilistically known (or unknown) time functions which affect the system behavior. Control variables are variables which may be manipulated by the manager. And, state variables are introduced to parameterize the set of input-output pairs in such a way as to achieve a unique dependence of the output on input and state. Since there are many ways in which a set of input-output pairs can be parametrized, the implication is that there are many ways in which an input-output relation can be cast into the form of an input-output-state relation. In other words, state variables in systems are defined entirely by the model constructed by the analyst. The definition of state variable is thus applicable only with respect to specific models.

Finally, the manager may establish designs of control systems not only on the basis of measures of effectiveness but also on the basis of the stability and the sensitivity of a system's trajectories. This is particularly the case if the managerial planning time is very large, and if measures of effectiveness are difficult to find. In such circumstances, "design" consists in selecting decision strategies which will respond to system disturbances in such a way as to return the system's time path to a specified time trajectory. While there may be many stabilizing decision strategies, managerial choice of strategies can be based on decision strategies having a prescribed degree of stability.

Planning under uncertainty but with a partially controlled environment occurs when actions taken by management influence the environment. For example, consider a monopolist making production and pricing decisions simultaneously. These decisions are inter-dependent. However, although classical economic theory assumes that given the price of a product a level of demand for that product will ensue (and vice-versa), in practice this is not the case. Instead, there is a probabilistic relationship between prices and demands. Thus, a change in price is found to have only a probabilistic, rather than a perfectly predictable effect upon demand. Similarly, although it is possible to influence pollution levels by controlling gas emissions from automobiles, the effects are probabilistic, because many other factors (such as atmospheric disturbances and turbulence) have unpredictable effects.

Planning under uncertainty with an uncontrolled environment occurs when no action by management can influence the nature of environmental disturbances. For example, consider a production manager, facing a demand for his product, who is in the short run unable to influence this demand. To make his productive facilities more manageable, he uses forecasting techniques to generate future expected demands. On the basis of these forecasts, and the costs in meeting these demands, he adopts production strategies which will both meet the demand and minimize costs. In more complicated situations, a production manager will also attempt to influence this uncertain demand for his product by advertising, promotion campaigns, and even price changes. As a result, he further integrates the functions of the firm in order to influence the environment and lessen the harmful effects of an unpredictable environment.

Planning under complete uncertainty (that is, in a completely random environment) occurs when we neither know nor are able to influence the environment. This category of planning problems is extremely important but difficult to analyze; important because most social and economic problems involve complete uncertainty, and difficult to analyze because there are no simple ways to investigate the effects of managerial courses of action. This is particularly the case over long periods of time, when all problems involve complete uncertainty. Thus, while the short run may be predictable in part, the long run is not. For this reason, when planning under complete uncertainty it is necessary that we construct mechanisms to improve our guesses about the behavior of the environment. In other words, subordinate intelligence-gathering systems are required to detect what, if any, changes occur in the environment. Whenever such changes are detected, decision mechanisms are developed to react to them. Because such planning problems are analytically and computationally very difficult to investigate, they will be considered only in general terms here.

When we plan under uncertainty, we implicitly consider several possible futures, each of which has its own probability of occurring. The various probabilities are weights which we determine arbitrarily by using a special model or by collecting and interpreting data in a special way. This is done entirely for convenience and is in reality not very meaningful, since only one future will in fact occur. This particular characterisitc of uncertainty gives rise to two modes of planning: (1) Planning conceived to meet expectations of future probabilistic states; this is called <u>average planning</u>.[5] (2) Planning conceived for a set of possible outcomes, given that one outcome will occur; this is called <u>contingency planning</u>. Contingency planning involves maintaining action programs which may be deployed if they become required. In contingency planning, costs of stored but unused capabilities must be compared with the costs and penalties of being unprepared to meet contingencies.[6]

Various examples of planning problems will be considered throughout the book. Below, we consider the problem of production planning. This problem is not only of considerable importance to managers but will also provide a source of examples demonstrating planning and control problems.

Example II.1: Production Planning

Production planning consists of (1) inventory control, (2) sales or demand forecasting, (3) production control and (4) capacity planning. Each of these problems can be investigated seperately or may be integrated as one simple system as described in Figure II.1.

Inventory and production decisions are, for the most part, reached in short term planning horizon; capacity planning decisions, however, are reached in a long range planning horizon. This difference in planning horizons is essentially due to the fact that capacity decisions involve considerably more risk than production decisions and their effects and side-effects are felt over longer periods to time. Sales and demand forecasting involve both short and long term planning horizons. When demand is forecasted to establish production plans, the forecast horizon is short; when it is capacity decisions, the forecast horizon is long.

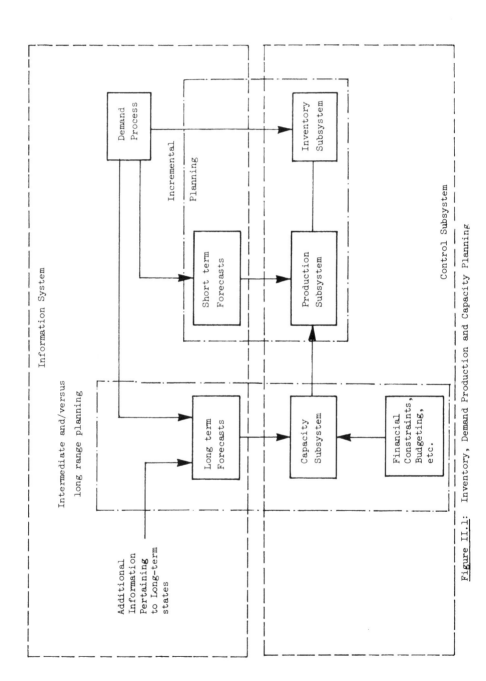

Figure II.1: Inventory, Demand Production and Capacity Planning

Decision	Goal(s)	Planning Time and Planning Mode	Information Inputs	Decision Structures	Comments	Decision Making Units
Capacity Expansion	Maximize rate of return, discounted profits	Several years, non-shifting long & intermediate planning	Long term demand forecasting technology forecasting etc.	Discrete at irregular intervals of time, single versus multiple expansion and time phasing of expansions, exports versus internal expansion	Considerations given to economies of scale, non-routine decision making	Top Management
Production Work Force	Minimize production costs, inventory costs. Demand satisfaction and operational efficiency criteria	One year or less, shifting incremental and intermediate planning	Inventory and demand short term forecasting	Continuous or discrete at small intervals of time. Open loop, feedback and constrained configuration.	Can be routinized by devising appropriate decision rules	Production Manager
Inventories	Minimize inventory ordering, holding shortage costs. Demand satisfying criteria	Short term incremental shifting planning. Planning time function of products characteristics and supplies	Short term demand forecasts	Discrete orders How much? When? How to order?	Routinized	Inventory Manager
Demand Estimation and forecasting	Minimize data collection costs, maximize usefulness of forecasting (least variance) mechanisms. Incorporate real-time information.	Shifting or non-shifting	Marketing intelligence, past data and records	Constrained or unconstrained configuration, on-line, real time information handling	Can be routinized after careful analysis of the demand and information handling process	Top to lower Management

TABLE II.1

Table II.1 outlines some of the goals, decisions, information inputs, decision structures and planning modes to be adopted. Notably a distinction in production capacity planning is made between shifting and non-shifting planning. Non-shifting planning consists of a fixed set of plans u(t) and assumes at a planning time $\tau = t_0$, that all decisions for $t_0 \leq \tau \leq T$ are made. Shifting-planning modes consist, on the other hand, in revising planned decisions when additional information is accumulated.

The nature and relevance of the planning mode is particularly acute when production and inventory are controlled on a real-time basis. Then, mechanisms for updating production decisions and inventory order plans are designed to incorporate relevant information as it becomes available.

Production managers tend to view the production system in Figure II.1 as a coherent whole. For practical purposes, however, the four problems indicated earlier may be separated, treating one problem's output as another's input.

The number of inventory and production problems one may consider is very large.[7] We shall therefore restrict ourselves to special cases of inventory and production control problems over time. These will emphasize: (1) Time variable and known demand models and (2) Time variables and stochastic demand models.

Capacity planning problems as opposed to inventory and production problems deal with increasing the productive capacity of a firm in response to anticipated demand growth. Given a known (or probabilistically determined) planning horizon, these decisions require a focus on two aspects of the problem. a. The size of the expansions and b. The timing of the expansions.

	Capacity Expansion	Production and Inventory Control
Time impact	over very long periods of time	over small periods of time
Uncertainty	we can rarely forecast with precision future demands	forecasts tend to be comparatively reliable
Decision cost	very expensive and irreversible. Involves a significant part of a firm's resources	comparatively inexpensive. A single error in production can be corrected in a latter period
Decision Structure	single or a stream of discrete expansions may be considered. Timing is important	repetitive, can be approximated by a continuous time path or by feedback decisions
Survival	the cost of being wrong is very large and can influence the survivability of the firm	the cost of being wrong is usually of no threat to the survival of the firm

TABLE II.2

Capacity expansion decisions incur present costs with the expectation of future returns over long periods of time and often require the comittment of a significant part of a firm's resources. Therefore, capacity expansions require that each decision be carefully evaluated. A chart distinguishing capacity expansion from production and inventory control is given in Table II.2.

Specific models of capacity expansion will be considered in Chapter V.

Having explained the functions and importance of planning, we now turn to establishing equations that represent the process of change. Such equations were called memory processes. In Section II.3 applications of such memory processes will be given.

II.2 Quantification of Memory Processes

Memory processes are those processes describing how past and anticipated states are related to, and affect present states.[8] Alternatively, we can state that evolution of present states, expressing a summary of past history and expected future states, can be described by a memory process. This memory process, as discussed in Chapter I, describes the residual effect of all past and expected events on the present.

Modeling a memory process, therefore becomes essential if a "view" of the past and of the expected "view" of the future are desired at a given present time. This "view" or summary of past and future is what we call the state of the system. In planning, a quantification of events (and their associated memory processes) are required for any rational

inferences of the future. Similarly, to influence the time paths of
specific states, in a desirable manner (i.e. control), it is necessary
that quantitative models of memory processes be defined. In this section,
we shall consider quantitative models which describe several classes of
memory processes. Specifically, we distinguish five types of memory
processes;[9] (1) No memory, (2) Differential memory, (3) Delay memory,
(4) Integro-differential memory, and (5) Anticipative memory. Each of
these processes may appear in a discrete or continuous form, depending on
the nature of the process and how it is modeled. A combination of these
memory processes can be used to construct more complex memories. Let us
now define, and consider examples of each of these processes.

(1) No memory

"No-memory" processes are defined when past and future states have no
effect on present states. Such processes are most common in static analyses
and characterize the relationship between sets of variables at one instant of
time. For example, a person unaware or uninformed of the past and with no
expectations of or information about the future is a person with "no memory".
Such a person will act on the basis of current information alone. An amnesia
victim would be an example. Time, ordinarily defined as a dimension along
which experience is recorded and anticipated, is simply not defined in such a
case. As another example, consider a young child. When a young child is hungry,
he cries. We cannot expect a child to estimate how much time has elapsed
since his last meal and cry whenever it is "time" to eat. Instead, the
child cries whenever he feels the pain of hunger, and this feeling is,

in a child's mind, independent of the time of the last meal. No-memory processes may also occur in business systems. Consider for example, the mechanism by which price and demand are related in a market. Assume that the relationship is expressed by a linear equation:

$$d(t) = a(t) + b(t)p(t)$$

where $d(t)$ = demand for a product at time t

$p(t)$ = price of the product at time t

$a(t), b(t)$ = parameters, function of time

This relationship describes the demand if the price is known at every instant of time. The effects of past and anticipated prices and demand, however, have no role in determining current price and demand. Therefore, at any one time, the demand $d(t)$ is found as a function of current variables only. A careful observation of the market mechanisms, however, will reveal that this model of price and demand is simplistic. Producers and consumers do have expectations about future prices and are aware of past prices and demand. In order to understand the effects of past and future conditions, more complex models of memory must be determined.

(2) Differential Memory

Differential memory is defined when the current state is only a function of the last state and other current variables (such as actions and disturbances). Therefore, past history is summarized in the last state attained and change is defined as an incremental process. A differential-memory mechanism is shown in Figure II.2. It is an extension of the no-memory mechanism outlined ealier. We now have a "memory" of past events summarized in one state which incorporates all past effects. This is still far short of our natural ability to recollect a string of past events simultaneously, but it is nonetheless a step toward making the past relevant to the present.

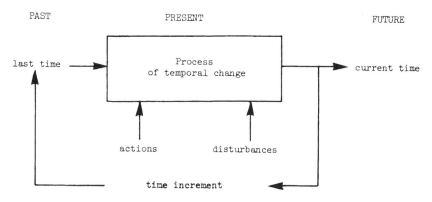

Figure II.2: Process of Temporal Change

Differential memory has important applications in business, economics and social problems. When there is a temporal recording of discrete events, we have what may be called a "difference-memory," characterized by discrete incremental changes in the state as a function of current variables.

For example, assume a production-inventory process where

I_t = inventory on hand at time t

P_t = production rate at time t

S_t = sales at time t

The production-inventory process can then be represented by a difference-memory process:

$$I_t - I_{t-1} = P_t - S_t$$

where the incremental change in inventory is measured by the inflow of products P_t, less the outflow S_t of products at a specific instant of time t. If the process is time-continuous, we replace subscripted variables by functions of time and at the limit we obtain a differential memory process:

$$dI(t)/dt = P(t) - S(t)$$

As another instance of difference memory, consider the example of demand and price given earlier (p. 68), and assume that demand is a linear function of both price and changes in prices. Then:

$$d_t = a_t + b_t p_t + c_t [p_t - p_{t-1}]$$

As the limit, this may be written in a differential form as:

$$d(t) = a(t) + b(t)p(t) + c(t)dp(t)/dt$$

That is, the demand is a function of price and incremental price changes.

Differential memory is, therefore, a mechanism for relating events at two successive instants of time. It holds for all past and future successive instants of time and thus allows us to reconstruct change. For example, returning to the equation given for the inventory-production process, we find that for a planning horizon of T periods:

$$
\begin{aligned}
I_1 - I_0 - P_1 + S_1 &= 0 \\
I_2 - I_1 \quad - P_2 + S_2 &= 0 \\
I_3 - I_2 \quad - P_3 + S_3 &= 0 \\
\cdot \quad \cdot \quad \cdot & \\
\cdot \quad \cdot \quad \cdot & \\
I_T - I_{T-1} \quad - P_t + S_T &= 0 \\
\hline
I_T \quad - I_0 - P_1 - \ldots - P_T + S_1 + \ldots + S_T &= 0
\end{aligned}
$$

That is, the change in inventory between times $t=T$ and $t=0$ equals the cumulation of all past production decisions P_t, written as:

$$P_1 + P_2 + \ldots + P_T = \sum_{t=0}^{T} P_t$$

less the cumulation of all past demand decisions S_t; or:

$$S_1 + S_2 + \ldots + S_T = \sum_{t=0}^{T} S_t$$

$$I_T - I_0 = \sum_{t=1}^{T} P_t - \sum_{t=1}^{T} S_t = \sum_{t=1}^{T} [P_t - S_t]$$

The final inventory at time T, I_T, is the sum of all past incremental changes, $P_t - S_t$, ($t = 1\ldots T$). If we consider the production-inventory process in continuous form, replacing the summation signs by integrals yields:

$$I(T) = I(0) + \int_0^T [P(t) - S(t)] dt$$

In other words, the inventory state at time T equals the initial inventory and the cumulative effects of all past changes on inventory.

(3) Delay Memory

Delay memory is defined when current states are functions of states which occurred τ periods in the past. This may occur when it takes time for the effects of certain events to be felt. For example, if a train leaves station A at time t and reaches station B at time $t+\tau$, a travel time of τ periods is involved. This travel time can be considered as a delay between the initiation of service (at time t in station A) and the fulfillment of that service (τ periods later in station B). As another example, assume that demand for a product at one instant of time is a function of the price of that product in the previous period:

$$d(t) = a(t-1) + b(t-1)p(t-1)$$

Then the process by which affects demand is a delayed process of one period. Delayed processes can be combined with differential-memory processes, in which case they may be called "differential-delay" processes. In such processes the effects of the delay are felt as a change in the state of a variable.

(4) Integro-Differential Memory

In differential-memory and delay-memory processes, as has been noted, past events can influence the present in two ways: first, there can be incremental changes; second, specific events in the past can influence current states. In integro-differential memory processes, current states are influenced by a time-dependent weighting function of past events. Deterioration of machines, for example, effects of advertising on sales, allocation of salesmen's effort in selling a product, complex price-demand relationship, and formation of capital can be described by integro-differential memory mechanisms. Assume that a salesman allocates a certain amount of effort to the sale of a product. Evidently, this allocation of effort has an effect not only on current sales but on future sales. In other words, results of sales efforts carry forward in time. However, each allocation of effort has a decreasing effectiveness in time, since buyers forget past efforts as time goes by. To generate sales, salesmen are required to call on buyers repeatedly to remind them and reinforce their willingness to buy. The allocation of sales effort in time[10] is an integro-differential memory process because the rate of change in sales can be affected by a function of current effort and the current effects of all past sales effort.

The general quantitative form of integro-differential memory processes is given by

$$dx(t)/dt = F\{a(t)x(t), \int_{-\infty}^{t} m(t,\tau)f(x(\tau),\tau)d\tau \}$$

In other words, the rate of change in the states $x(t)$ at some time t is a function τ of the current states plus a weighting $m(t,\tau)$ of functions F of the states at all past instants of time. The role of the weighting function is an extremely important one, as it reflects the present relative importance of an event that has occurred at a specific instant of time in the past. Although the quantitative formulation of this memory process is complicated, appropriate modeling of such memory processes would seek relevant and functional forms for F and f that are mathematically tractable.

(5) Anticipative Memory

Anticipative memory is defined when current states are also functions of future states. In other words, the anticipation of future states influences current states and current levels of activity. The importance of such a memory mechanism for social science is great.[11] As individuals we face an essentially unknown future; man's activities--and indeed his existence -- are a function of this future. The "moment in being," which is the locus of our every actual and potential experience, our every thought, feeling, decision, and action, cannot be separated from our anticipation.[12]

Anticipating the future is an activity in which we are continually involved. The indeterminate nature of the future and our need to organize and confront this future make it essential that we anticipate. Just as we attempt to analyze an unknown statistical population by sampling, so we try to predict the future (see Table II.3).

	Method of study	Subject of study
Statistical Analysis	Sampling	Statistical population
Prediction	Anticipation	Future

Table II.3: Statistical Analysis and Prediction of the Future

However, while the theory of statistics and statistical inference is well developed (to the extent that rational and acceptable inference of a statistical population is possible), methods of anticipation are to a far greater extent intuitive or based on experience rather than on a theoretical foundation.

The main difference between inference by statistical sampling and anticipating the future is that statistical populations change in time, so that although a statistical description of an environment is true for one instant of time, it may not be true for another. The mechanisms which control change are themselves altered over time. For short periods of time, however, it is reasonable to assume that these control mechanisms do not change and that therefore the future is merely an extension of the present.

Let us consider speculation in the stock market as an example of anticipation. It sometimes happens that expectation of a price rise in the future, or of the existence of conditions favorable to a stock prompt us to take a present action which is a result of neither past history nor of current conditions. Of course, the past is an important influence on our expectations of a future price, but past prices have little weight compared with our "intrapolation" of the future -- i.e., the mechanism by which a set of future uncertain events is related to the present. Such anticipative processes can be quantified only speculatively. If it is assumed that effects of the future on the present can be represented by a weighted sum of future states $x(\tau)$, and $\tau > t$, then:

$$\frac{dx(t)}{dt} = \{a(t)x(t), \; \Xi \int_t^\infty m(t,\tau)f(x(\tau), t)d\tau \} \quad (3.8)$$

where t is the present time; $m(t,\tau)$ is a function (probabilistic or not) weighting a function f of future states $x(\tau)$; $\int_t^\infty \ldots d\tau$ is the cumulative effect of the future on the present, and Ξ is a function describing the process of change. In other words, quantitative modeling of the process by which an expectation is formed (that is, the process of anticipation) involves a forecast of the future, a weighting of the future, and a function describing the change in expectation.

Modeling memory processes is a difficult task, but it is necessary if we want to model, manipulate, and possibly control change. Examples of how certain business and operational "memory processes" can be constructed are considered next.

II.3 Memory Processes - Mathematical Examples

In this section we consider mathematical examples of memory processes which will be extended further in Chapters III and IV.

Example II.2: Elementary techniques of forecasting demand.

The demand for a product is an essential piece of information for a manufacturer, without which production planning and inventory control become extremely difficult. For the most part, however, the demand is unknown, and manufacturers seek mechanisms by which they can estimate it. Here, two simple techniques for estimating demand will be described:[13] moving averages and exponential smoothing. These are popular in the practice of management science, and are examples of a differential memory process.

The technique of moving averages considers all past instants as being equally representative of the past. Therefore, if d_t are observed demands at some instant of time t, and D_t is the current average demand, then

$$D_t = \frac{d_t + d_{t-1} + \ldots + d_{t-(N-1)}}{N}$$

is used for estimating the future demand. It is evident that this equation can be rearranged to yield:

$$D_t = D_{t-1} + \frac{1}{N}(d_t - D_{t-N})$$

which is a simple memory difference process. Here the oldest (d_{t-N}) and newest (d_t) demand observations have the same importance. To avoid this, we introduce a mechanism weighting past observations according to how recent they are. That is, if $m_o, m_1 \ldots m_{N-1}$ is a set of such weights and

$$\sum_{i=0}^{N-1} m_i = 1$$

then a weighted average would be

$$D_t = m_o d_t + m_1 d_{t-1} + \ldots + m_{N-1} d_{t-N-1}$$

or

$$D_t = \sum_{i=0}^{N-1} m_{N-i} d_{t-(N-i)}$$

A continuous time analogue to this equation (with $N = t$) is;

$$D(t) = \int_0^t m(t-\tau)d(\tau)d\tau + D(0)m(t)$$

If we let $m(t) = e^{-\delta t}$ and

taking derivatives in $D(t)$ with respect to time yields

$$\frac{dD(t)}{dt} = \delta [d(t) - D(t)]$$

This equation is called the continuous exponential smoothing method The discrete-time equivalent is written as:

$$D_t = (1-\delta)D_{t-1} + \delta d_t$$

where δ is known as the "weighting" or "smoothing" constant and is a value between zero and one.

Example II.3 Advertising: Forgetting and Recall.

In several studies of advertising[14] it has been assumed that advertising is in effect an investment in "goodwill." In other words, if $G(t)$ is a quantity describing the willingness of consumers to buy a product, by spending $a(t)$ advertising dollars at time t we will increase the willingness of the consumers(some increasing function of $G(t)$) to buy the product. Nerlove and Arrow [40] assumed that the rate of change in goodwill is given by:

$$dG(t)/dt = a(t) - \delta G(t)$$

That is, the rate of change in goodwill is proportionate to the amount $a(t)$ of dollars spent on advertising, less a deterioration rate $\delta G(t)$. There are assumed to be opposing forces at work: those which increase goodwill — advertising; and those which over time, decrease goodwill — forgetting.[15] We can show, as in example II.2, that the differential memory process of $G(t)$ is a special case of :

$$G(t) = \int_{-\infty}^{t} m(t-\tau)a(\tau)d\tau$$

with $m(t)$ an exponential function. Of course by changing the weighting function $m(t)$, alternative representations of the evolution of goodwill can be found.

Example II.4: Transportation Over Time

The classical transportation problem (see Figure II.3) consists in finding a set of transport decisions x_{ij} from source i to destination j (i=1,...n; j=1,..m) such that the cost of transportation is minimized. This problem is widely applicable in management science and logistics to which we shall return in Chapter III.[16] Here, it will be shown how a static transportation problem can be transformed into a dynamic one. By making this transformation, we can specifically introduce the time dimension into decisions regarding transportation. A set of transportation decisions must include:

Supply equations: $\sum_{j=1}^{m} x_{ij} = a_i \quad i=1,\ldots n$

Demand equations: $\sum_{i=1}^{n} x_{ij} = b_j \quad j=1,\ldots m$

$$\sum_{i=1}^{n} a_i = \sum_{j=1}^{m} b_j$$

In other words, the sum of all transported quantities x_{ij} from a particular source i to all possible destinations $j(j=1,\ldots m)$ equals the available supply a_i. Similarly, the quantity received at a specific destination j from all possible sources i $(i=1\ldots n)$ equals the demand b_j at the destination. Since there are no losses in the transportation network, the sum of all quantities x_{ij} sent from sources i is necessarily equal to the sum of all quantities received. This is expressed by $\Sigma a_i = \Sigma b_j$.

Transportation decisions are not made all at one time, of course. Rather, managers face a variety of constraints, such as route capacities and transportation capacities, to which they must conform. A quantity x_{ij} at time t is therefore more appropriately given as $x_{ij}(t)$. Furthermore, a supply a_i in some source is not exhausted instantaneously. Management takes steps to ensure that the rate at which supply is exhausted is carefully planned to allow smooth and efficient operations. The static model above is therefore no longer appropriate; instead, if we define by $\sum_{j=1}^{m} x_{ij}(t)$, and $\sum_{i=1}^{n} x_{ij}(t)$ that change of quantities <u>transported</u> from i to all j, and the change in quantities <u>received</u> from all i in j, then the change $\Delta y_i(t)$ in source i at time t is:

$$\Delta y_i(t) = y_i(t) - y_i(t - \Delta t)$$

And the change $\Delta z_j(t)$ in destination j at time t is:

$$\Delta z_j(t) = z_j(t) - z_j(t - \Delta t)$$

where

$$y_i(t) - y_i(t-\Delta t) = -(\sum_{j=1}^{m} x_{ij}(t))\Delta t \qquad i=1,\ldots n$$

$$z_j(t) - z_j(t-\Delta t) = +(\sum_{i=1}^{n} x_{ij}(t))\Delta t \qquad j=1,\ldots m$$

When time is continuous, this is reduced to:

$$dy_i(t)/dt = -\sum_{j=1}^{m} x_{ij}(t) \qquad i=1,\ldots n$$

$$dz_j(t)/dt = +\sum_{i=1}^{n} x_{ij}(t) \qquad j=1,\ldots m$$

At the initial time, sources are "full" (i.e. containing a_i), while destinations are "empty" (i.e., containing nothing). When transport decisions are completed at a time T, however, the sources are "empty" while destinations are "full" (i.e, containing b_j). This is translated into the following conditions:

$$y_i(0) = a_i \qquad\qquad y_i(T) = 0 \qquad i=1,\ldots n$$

$$z_j(0) = 0 \qquad\qquad z_j(T) = b_j \qquad j=1,\ldots m$$

$$\sum_{i=1}^{n} a_i = \sum_{j=1}^{m} b_j$$

In such a formulation, transportation between a source and a destination is assumed to be instantaneous. This, of course, need not be the case; instead, a travel time of τ_{ij} periods between sources i and destinations j can be considered. To account for travel time τ_{ij} in our equations, we introduce time delays, obtaining the following equations:

$$dy_i(t)/dt = - \sum_{j=1}^{m} x_{ij}(t)$$

$$dz_j(t)/dt = + \sum_{i=1}^{n} x_{ij}(t-\tau_{ij})$$

At the initial time t=0 and at the final time t=T; we also have:[17]

$$y_i(0) = a_i \qquad x_i(T - \max_j \tau_{ij}) = 0 \qquad i=1,\ldots n$$

$$z_j(0) = 0 \qquad z_j(T - \min_i \tau_{ij}) = b_j \qquad j=1,\ldots m$$

$$\sum_{i=1}^{n} a_i = \sum_{j=1}^{m} b_j$$

Because of the time delays, the equations just derived are cumbersome; they should be transformed into a simpler form, as follows:

$$y_i(t) = a_i - \sum_{j=1}^{m} w_{ij}(t)$$

$$z_j(t) = \sum_{i=1}^{n} w_{ij}(t-\tau_{ij})$$

Rewriting the dynamic transport equations we obtain:

$$dw_{ij}(t)/dt = x_{ij}(t)$$

$$w_{ij}(0) = 0, \quad i,j \text{ and } t \in [-\tau_{ij}, 0] \qquad 18$$

and

$$\sum_{j=1}^{n} w_{ij}(T-\tau_{ij}) = a_i \qquad \sum_{i=1}^{n} w_{ij}(T-\tau_{ij}) = b_j$$

$$\sum_{i=1}^{n} a_i = \sum_{j=1}^{m} b_j$$

In this equation, $w_{ij}(t)$ is the cumulative utilization of route ij at time t. By superimposing transportation constraints on the model, we obtain the transportation capacity C:

$$0 \leq \sum_{i=1}^{n} \sum_{j=1}^{m} x_{ij}(t) \leq C$$

and the route capacity c_{ij} between i and j:

$$0 \leq x_{ij}(t) \leq c_{ij}$$

Other constraints may be constructed, expressing the ability to transport at particular times.

The importance of the transportation problem over time is shown by its many applications, which will be indicated in Chapter III. The explicit inclusion of the time dimension in transportation allows the planning of transportation schedules-- that is, it permits transportation capability over time--and provides a solution to logistical distribution problems, in which the essential task is to deliver goods on time subject to constraints on transportation capability.

A comparison between the "static" and "dynamic" transportation problems (see Table II.4) indicates that these address themselves to different areas: the static problem is a special and an extremely limited case of the dynamic problem.

	STATIC	DYNAMIC
Memory	No memory of past transport decisions	Has memory of past transport decisions
Decision Mode	Simultaneity of transportation decisions at one time	Simultaneity and sequentiality of transportation decisions
Role of Planning Horizon	Non-existent (myopic)	Evaluate the future needs for transportation and incorporate them in the present (non-myopic)

Table II.4: Transportation: Static and Dynamic

Example II.5 A Machine's Salvage Value- Differential Memory

We persue section I.5.(2) and assume that a machine bought at an instant of time t, costs $K. The machine's salvage value- i.e. its resale value- is given by S(t). The rate of change of the salvage value is a function of the deterioration of the machine and the maintenance policy employed. The memory process describing the evolution of the machine's salvage value can be simply given by,

$$dS(t)/dt = -a(t) + f(t)m(t) \qquad S(0) = K$$

where

   S(t) = salvage value of the machine at time t($)

   m(t) = maintenance policy-hours of maintenance at time t

   f(t) = maintenance effectiveness function at time t-$ added to S(t)/hours, of maintenance.

   a(t) = "obsolescence function" at time t-$ subtracted from S(t)

Such a model has been used by Thompson (76) to determine an optimum maintenance policy. A probabilistic version of this model will be considered in section II.5, and the optimum maintenance policy obtained in Chapter IV.

Numerous other examples of memory processes are included as problems and exercises at the end of this chapter. Next, we turn to establishing a quantitative basis for probabilistic memory processes.

II.4 Probabilistic Memory- Stochastic Processes

Previously, we assumed that the evolution of processes is described by difference or differential equations. Given a differential equation for example, integration of this equation- analytically or numerically- could lead to a time path. This is a pair {x,t} which we wrote as a function x(t). The pair {x,t} was thus far assumed known. That is, given t, a corresponding value x could be defined by integration of the differential equation (see the Appendix at the end of this chapter). Often, however, the evolution of processes is subject to influences which cannot be described with certainty. In other words, our partial knowledge of the evolution of processes prevents us from determining how the pair {x,t} evolves, by straight mathematical means. As is common in statistics, we substitute our lack of knowledge concerning {x,t} by assuming that x is a random variable with probability distribution $F(x,t)$. Knowledge of the time-path {x,t} is then expressed in our ability to describe:

(1) The evolution of the probability parameters of {x,t}. For example, the evolution of the mean, variance, and other moments of x describes a state of knowledge concerning the time-path {x,t}.

(2) The evolution of the function forms of the probability distributions $F(x,t)$. For example, if for all t, $F(x,t)$ is known to be a normal probability distribution, then we would have described a certain property of the time-path {x,t}. Time paths, defined by pairs {x(t); t≥0} where $x(t) = \{x,t\}$ are a family of random variables, are called stochastic processes. Stochastic processes are extremely important in the study of management science processes. For example, when we say that the demand for a product is a stochastic process, we essentially state that the demand time path of the product can be characterized by a family of random variables whose evolution we may be able to model. Similarly, we have repeatedly stated that management over time involves uncertainties concerning the future which cannot be dismissed when we are planning a present or future course of action. To account for this uncertainty, it is necessary that the "sources of uncertainty," i.e., the random influences, be identified and incorporated in a model describing the evolution of the random variable x(t). Given this model it is still required to determine

criteria for decision making which reflect our attitude towards future outcomes. In this section, we shall describe certain families of stochastic processes and consider some of their applications in modeling management processes. In Chapter V, we shall indicate approaches for describing the evolution of the moments, as well as the probability distributions, of the stochastic processes and because this is a broad and important field, the reader is referred to references at the end of this chapter for further study.[19]

The theory of stochastic processes has its origin in the study of the kinetic behavior of molecules in gas by physicists in the 19th century. It is only in the last few decades, following works by Einstein, Kolmogorov, Levy, Ornstein and Uhlenbeck, Wiener, and others[20] that stochastic processes have been studied in some depth. These scientists were concerned with a particular group of processes called Brownian motion. These and other processes will be described next.

First, we shall define some properties of stochastic processes which are required for any meaningful applications. Namely, stationary and non-stationary as well as ergodic and non-ergodic stochastic processes will be contrasted. Thereafter, models of "Random Walk," "Brownian Motion," "Markov Processes," Poisson Processes, stochastic difference and stochastic integral equations and differential equations will be defined and applied to the study of processes occurring over time. Throughout the chapter we shall adopt the convention that $m(t)$ and $v(t)$ denote the mean and variance of a stochastic process. Greek letters such as $\xi(t)$ and $\eta(t)$ will denote sources of uncertainty.

(1) Properties of Stochastic Processes.

Stationarity: Assume that $f(x,t)$ is a probability distribution of the random variable x at time t. The statistical characteristics of this stochastic process-expressed in the evolution of the mean and variance-is given by:

$$m(t) = E[x(t)] = \int_{-\infty}^{\infty} xf(x,t)dx$$

$$v(t) = \text{var } x(t) = \int_{-\infty}^{\infty} (x-m(t))^2 f(x,t)dx$$

where $m(t)$ and $v(t)$ are the time-variant mean and variance of $f(x,t)$. Assume that the probability distribution is not a function of time. That is

$$f(x,t) = f(x;t+\tau) = f(x) \qquad \text{for all t and } \tau$$

This property is called strict stationarity. Consider now, the joint probability distribution of two random variables x_1 and x_2. Their probability distribution $f(x_1,x_2; t_1,t_2)$ describes a stationary stochastic process if;

$$f(x_1,x_2; t_1,t_2) = f(x_1,x_2; t_1 + \tau, t_2 + \tau)$$

If we consider two instants of time t_1 and $t_2 = t_1 + \tau$, this can be written as:

$$f(x_1,x_2;t_1,t_2) = f(x_1,x_2;t_1,t_1+\tau) = f(x_1,x_2;t_2-t_1) = f(x_1,x_2;\tau)$$

That is, for the joint distribution of a strict stationary process, the distribution is not a function of time, but a function of the time difference τ between the two random variables. As a result, the correlation function $B(t_1,t_2)$, describing the correlation between x_1 and x_2 at instants of time t_1 and t_2, will be found to be a function of the time difference $t_2 - t_1 = \tau$. Namely,

$$B(t_1,t_2) = \text{covariance } (x_1,x_2;t_1,t_2)$$

$$B(t_1,t_2) = \int_{-\infty}^{\infty} \int_{-\infty}^{\infty} x_1 x_2 f(x_1,x_2;t_1, t_2) dx_1 dx_2$$

The autocovariance function, describing the correlation function about the means is given by : $K(t_1, t_2)$ where

$$K(t_1, t_2) = \text{autocovariance } (x_1, x_2; t_1, t_2)$$

$$K(t_1, t_2) = B(t_1, t_2) - E[x_1(t_1)] E[x_2(t_2)]$$

where $E[\cdot]$ denotes the expectation operator.

The correlation coefficient $R_1(\tau)$ of the random variable x_1, function of the time difference τ is

$$R_1(\tau) = \frac{\text{cov } \{x_1(t) \, x_1(t+\tau)\}}{\text{var } \{x_1(t)\} \text{ var } \{x_1(t+\tau)\}}$$

Because of the stationarity $\text{var}\{x(t)\} = \text{var}\{x(t+\tau)\}$ and so

$$R(\tau) = [B(\tau) - m^2]/\text{var}(x(t)) = K(\tau)/K(0)$$

That is, the correlation coefficient $R(\tau)$ is a function of the time difference $\tau = t_2 - t_1$ only.

Ergodicity: An ergodic process is a process whose time average equals the mean of the random process. For example, say that $x(t)$ is a random process. The average $\bar{x}$ is given by

$$\bar{x} = \lim_{T \to \infty} (1/T) \int_0^T x(t) dt$$

Since $\bar{x}$ is time independent, (because t is integrated out of the integral above), $m(t)$ must similarly be time independent. In other words,

$$m(t) = E\{x(t)\} = m$$

Further, if the process has the property that:

$$\text{Prob } [m = \bar{x}] = 1$$

then it is called an ergodic process. Since m is now the average, its variance must be zero as time goes to infinity. Thus.

$$E\{(1/T^2) \int_0^T \int_0^T (x(t_1)-m)(x(t_2)-m)dt_1 dt_2\} =$$

$$= (1/T^2) \int_0^T \int_0^T [E(x(t_1))E(x(t_2)) - m^2] dt_1 dt_2$$

where $B(t_1,t_2) = E(x(t_1)x(t_2))$ is the correlation function. That is

$$\lim_{T \to \infty} (1/T^2) \int_0^T \int_0^T [B(t_1,t_2) - m^2] dt_1 dt_2 = 0$$

This last equation and the time invariance of m provide the necessary and sufficient conditions for time invariance of the random processes x(t). Since an ergodic process is necessarily stationary, (the opposite is not true, a stationary process need not be ergodic), we have $B(t_2,t_1) = B(t_2-t_1)$. A change of variables $\tau = t_2-t_1$ and integration of the integral above indicates that

$$\lim_{T \to \infty} (1/T) \int_0^T (1-\tau/T)(B(\tau)-m^2)d\tau < \infty$$

Stationary and Independent Increments: An increment $\Delta x(t)$,

$$\Delta x(t) = x(t+\Delta t) - x(t)$$

is a stationary and independent increment if $\Delta x(t)$ is a stationary random process and if $\Delta x(t)$ and $\Delta x(s)$ are statistically independent. This property of random increments is an extremely important one and leads to well known processes such as Poisson, Wiener, etc. as will soon be seen.

Stationarity, ergodicity and independent increments of time are properties which are sometimes necessary for the mathematical tractability of stochastic processes. In the next section, we consider specific models of such processes, the most important ones being the random walk and brownian motion. Of course, these models are extremely simple compared to the actual behavior and evolution of social and business processes. However, they do provide a first approximation.

(2) Random Walk Models

Consider a line and assume that a point is positioned on this line (Figure II.3). The point can move to the right or to the left. For example, if we define by P(t) the probabilistic

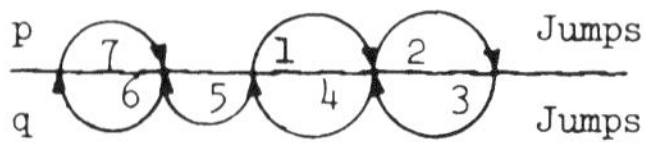

Figure II.3: An Unrestriced Random Walk

price of a product at time t, we may postulate that

$$P(t) = P(t-\Delta t) + \xi(t)$$

where $\xi(t)$ is a source of uncertainty defined by;

$$\xi(t) = \begin{cases} +\Delta P & \text{with probability } p \\ -\Delta P & \text{with probability } 1-p \end{cases}$$

In other words, the price at time t equals the price in the previous period $t-\Delta t$ plus a random movement of the price. This random movement consists in a price increase ΔP with probability p and a price decrease with probability q (= 1-p). Letting the price P(t) be the position on the line at time t, ΔP are the jumps expressing price increases and decreases.

Suppose that we consider not one but a series of n jumps $x_1, x_2, \ldots, x_n$ where we replace $\xi(t)$ by x_t and ΔP by 1. The sum S_n equals

$$S_n = \sum_{i=1}^{n} x_i$$

where
$$\text{Prob}\{x_i = +1\} = p$$
$$\text{Prob}\{x_i = -1\} = q$$
$$p + q = 1$$

That is, if we define the line in Figure II.3 by a set of points $\ldots -2, -1, 0, 1, 2, \ldots$, and letting "i" be one of these points, the last equation can be written as

$$P_{i,i+1} = p \qquad P_{i,i-1} = q$$

In other words, the probability of jumping to "i+1" or "i-1", given that we are in "i", is given by p and q respectively. Each jump is assumed to be independent, and therefore the probability of jumping from i to j in n jumps $P_{ij}^{(n)}$ can be described by a binomial probability distribution,

$$P_{ij}^{(n)} = \text{Prob}\{x_1 + \ldots + x_n = j-i\} =$$

$$\binom{n}{\frac{n+j-i}{2}} p^{\left[\frac{n+j-1}{2}\right]} q^{\left[\frac{n-j+1}{2}\right]}$$

The mean and variance of this distribution are given by

$E(j-1) = n(p-q)$

$\text{var}(j-i) = 4npq$

The process we have just described is called an <u>unrestricted random walk</u>, and it describes the random movement of a point on an unrestricted line. Inserting restrictions on the number of positions and on the probabilities of jumps will lead to different random walk models. These will be considered later on. The random movement of a particle on a line-i.e. the random walk model- has been used (because of analytical tractability) in the modeling of the probabilistic evolution of economic variables. It makes however, implicit assumptions which are worth pointing out. For example, the random walk model of prices' evolution described earlier makes specific assumptions concerning the process of change. This process is timeless-i.e. it does not change in time. Thus, if the price of a commodity at some instant of time t is $P(t)$ then at an instant of time Δt later the price can be only; $P(t) \pm \Delta P$.

Finally, the evolution of prices is entirely independent of the prices' past history (since price at one instant of time depends only on the price at the previous instant of time). Such assumptions, compared to the real economic and social processes we face are extremely simplistic. They are required however, if we are to gain a measure of analytical tractability. As a larger measure of realism is introduced in the models, their analytical tractability is correspondingly less difficult. The stringency of the assumptions required to construct probabilistic models over time thus indicates that these can be useful to study systems which exhibit small variations in time. Models with large and unpredictable variations must be based on an intuitive understanding of the problem at hand and the choice of appropriate courses of action based on "managerial wisdom".

We shall next define continuous random walk models. These models are a limit of the discrete random walks. That is, points on the line no longer jump to integer points but to neighboring points. Continuous random walk models will lead to a partial differential equation[21] called the Kolmogorov [22] or the Fokker-Plank[23] equation. A solution of this equation will yield the probability distribution of the random variable $x(t)$ at time t. To obtain the Fokker-Plank equation we reconsider the movement of the particle on the line and denote the state x of the point at time t by a function $f(x,t)$. At time $t+\Delta t$

$$f(x,t+\Delta t) = pf(x-\Delta x,t) + qf(x + \Delta x,t)$$

That is, the probability of being in x at $t+\Delta t$ equals the probability p of jumping Δx and of being in $x-\Delta x$ plus the probability $q(=1-p)$

of jumping $-\Delta x$ and of being in $x+\Delta x$, both in the time interval Δt. Replacing $f(x, t+\Delta t)$, $f(x-\Delta x,t)$ and $f(x+\Delta x,t)$ by Taylor series approximations, about $f(x,t)$;

$$f(x, t+\Delta t) = f(x,t) + \Delta t \frac{\partial f(x,t)}{\partial t} + O(\Delta t)^2$$

$$f(x-\Delta x, t) = f(x,t) - \Delta x \frac{\partial f(x,t)}{\partial x} + \frac{1}{2}(\Delta x)^2 \frac{\partial^2 f(x,t)}{\partial x^2} + O(\Delta x)^3$$

$$f(x+\Delta x, t) = f(x,t) + \Delta x \frac{\partial f(x,t)}{\partial x} + \frac{1}{2}(\Delta x)^2 \frac{\partial^2 f(x,t)}{\partial x^2} + O(\Delta x)^3$$

will yield a second order partial differential equation:

$$\frac{\partial f}{\partial t} = -(p-q)\frac{\Delta x}{\Delta t}\frac{\partial f}{\partial x} + \frac{1}{2}\frac{(\Delta x)^2}{\Delta t}\frac{\partial^2 f}{\partial x^2} + O(\Delta t)^2 + O(\Delta x)^3$$

where Δx, Δt, $O(\Delta t)^2$ and $O(\Delta x)^3$ are very small. For the equation of $f(x,t)$ to make sense, it is clearly required that there exists limits to $\Delta x/\Delta t$ and $(\Delta x)^2/\Delta t$ as both Δx and Δt tend to zero. Specifically, we write

$$\lim_{\Delta x \to 0, \Delta t \to 0} (\Delta x)^2/\Delta t = 2D$$

where D is a constant called the drift of the process. Similarly, by writing

$$\lim_{\Delta x \to 0, \Delta t \to 0} (p-q)\Delta x/\Delta t = 2C$$

where C is also a constant called the instantaneous mean of the process. Intuitively, 2C indicates the mean speed at which the point moves on the line, while D is the instantaneous variance of the process.

Using these limits, we note that the probability of jumping on the line is then;

$$p = \frac{1}{2} + \frac{C}{2D} \Delta x \quad , \quad q = \frac{1}{2} - \frac{C}{2D} \Delta x$$

This is found by multiplying 2C by Δx and replacing $(\Delta x)^2/\Delta t$ by 2D.

Neglecting the terms in $O(\Delta t)^2$ and $O(\Delta x)^3$ in the partial differential equation of $f(x,t)$, we obtain:

$$\frac{\partial f(x,t)}{\partial t} = -2C \frac{\partial f(x,t)}{\partial x} + D \frac{\partial^2 f(x,t)}{\partial x^2}$$

This is called the Fokker-Plank partial differential (or the diffusion) equation. It can now be shown easily that a normal probability distribution with mean $m(t)$ and variance $v(t)$

$$m(t) = 2Ct \quad , \quad v(t) = 2Dt$$

solves this equation. That is,

$$f(x,t) = [1/(2\pi v(t))^{1/2}] \exp[-\frac{1}{2} \frac{(x-m(t))^2}{v(t)}]$$

Using a similar procedure, other random walk models will be constructed. We may distinguish between random walk models with one or two absorbing barriers as well as reflecting barriers. For example, when a point x=o is reached, the random walk model terminates (i.e p_{00}=1) and we remain in that point, then we have an absorbing barrier.

Similarly, a reflecting barrier expresses the notion that when a reflecting point is reached, we are automatically "reflected" back into the line.

Generalizing the partial differential equations of random walk models, we state that the probability distribution describing the evolution of x over time is given by the solution of the general Fokker-Plank (diffusion) equation;

$$\frac{\partial f}{\partial t} = -\frac{\partial}{\partial x}[a(x,t)f(x,t)] + \frac{1}{2}\frac{\partial^2}{\partial x^2}[b(x,t)f(x,t)]$$

Here $a(x,t)$ and $b(x,t)$, although functions of x and time t, describe as 2C and 2D above, the instantaneous mean speed of a point on the line and the instantaneous variance of this movement. The solution for $f(x,t)$ when $a(x,t)$, $b(x,t)$ are non-linear for example is extremely difficult, and to date only special simple cases such as $a(x,t) = a(t)x$, $b(x,t)=b(t)x$ have been solved. In applications of system optimization under uncertainty, however, it may be sufficient to determine the evolution of probability moments rather than the distributions themselves. For example, suppose $\{x,t; t \geq 0\}$ is a stochastic process for which $f(x,t)$ above represents the probability distribution of the variable $x(t)$. Then, we may write the mean and variance functions for the given stochastic process as $m(t)$ and $v(t)$ and seek from the Fokker-Plank diffusion equation, the differential equations describing the evolutions of these probability moments.

Methods for describing the evolution probability moments may be found by the use of generating functions.[24] In particular, characteristic functions, probability generating functions and other transform methods will be introduced and used in Chapter V.

(3) The Wiener-Levy Process (or Brownian Motion)

The general Fokker-Plank equation described above provides a model for a large class of stochastic processes. Of historical as well as practical importance is the Brownian Motion, also called the Wiener-Levy process.

The process has its origin in a study of Robert Brown, a Botanist, who observed in 1828 that small particles immersed in a liquid perform irregular (random) movements. Subsequently, Einstein at the beginning of this century suggested a mathematical description for the movement of these particles which was studied further by Wiener and Levy and is now called the Wiener-Levy process. Specifically, a stochastic process $\{x(t); t \geq 0\}$ is defined as a Wiener-Levy process if

(a) $x(t)$ is a stationary independent increment process

(b) For each t and τ,

$$E\{x(t) - x(\tau)\} = 0$$
$$E\{x(t) - x(\tau)\}^2 = 2D|t-\tau|, \; t, \tau \geq 0$$

where $2D$ is a constant.

As discussed in section II.4.(1), (see p. 32), an independent increment process is defined when each two increments of times Δt and $\Delta \tau$, $\Delta x(t)$ (= $x(t+\Delta t) - x(t)$) and $\Delta x(\tau)$ (= $x(\tau+\Delta t) - x(\tau)$), are statistically independent. Einstein was able to show that a process with the properties (a) and (b) above has normal distribution with zero mean and variance $2Dt$. Therefore,

$$f(x,t) = \frac{1}{\sqrt{2\pi D t}} \exp(-x^2/2Dt)$$

which is a unique solution of the Fokker-Plank Equation given by;

$$\frac{\partial f(x,t)}{\partial t} = D \frac{\partial^2 f(x,t)}{\partial x^2}$$

$$f(x,0) = 0 \quad \text{for} \quad x \neq 0$$

(4) The Markov Process

The random walk and Wiener-Levy processes discussed above belong to a large and important **class** of processes said to have a Markov property. Markov processes have the property that at any time t, the state of the process depends on the immediately preceding state or states. Specifically, a stochastic process $\{x(t); t \geq 0\}$, is a Markov process if for each finite set of times $t_1, t_2, \ldots, t_n, t_{n+1}$ ($t_{i+1} > t_i$), the conditional probability distribution of $x(t_{n+1})$ depends on the state at the previous instant. That is

$$\text{Prob}\{x(t_{n+1}) | x(t_1), \ldots, x(t_n)\} = \text{Prob}\{x(t_{n+1}) | x(t_n)\}$$

Thus value of previous states determines the next state. Let us consider an interval of time Δt. In this interval, $x(t)$ can take on a finite set of values $\{s_1, s_2, \ldots, s_n\}$. The probability for moving from state s_i to state s_j is given by $\text{Prob}\{s_j/s_i\}$ and is known as the transition probability. For all states s_i ($i = 1, \ldots, n$) we define a matrix P:

$$P_{ij} = \text{Prob}\{s_j/s_i\}$$

	$s_1, \ldots, s_n$
s_1	$p_{11} \ldots p_{1n}$
$\vdots$	$\vdots \quad \vdots$
s_n	$p_{n1} \ldots p_{nn}$

Graphically, the **matrix** P is given in Figure II.4.

When we are at a state i, for example, we may move to any one of the other states s_j ($s_j \neq s_i$) or remain in state s_i. Therefore,

$$\sum_{j=1}^{n} p_{ij} = 1 \qquad p_{ij} \geq 0$$

Consider now a succession of time intervals $\Delta t, 2\Delta t, \ldots, n\Delta t$ and assume that the transition probabilities p_{ij} do not change in time (i.e., they are stationary). Further, let $[p_{ij}^m]$ be the transition probabilities in m time intervals. For a Markov process, this transition probability depends on the previous (m-1)th time interval. That is

$$p_{ij}^m = p_{i1}^{m-1} p_{1j} + p_{i2}^{m-1} p_{2j} + \ldots + p_{in}^{m-1} p_{nj}$$

or

$$p_{ij}^m = \sum_{k=1}^{n} p_{ik}^{m-1} p_{kj}$$

This is called the Chapman-Kolmogorov recurrence equation describing the evolution of transition probabilities in m-steps. It can also be written as;

$$p_{ij}^m = \sum_{k=1}^{n} p_{ik} p_{kj}^{m-1}$$

The unconditional probability that we may be at stage j at time $m(\Delta t)$ is therefore

$$p_j^m = \sum_{k=1}^{n} p_k^{m-1} p_{kj}$$

Since the transition in k time intervals is given by

$$p_{ij}^k = \sum_{r=1}^{m} p_{ir}^s p_{rj}^{k-s}$$

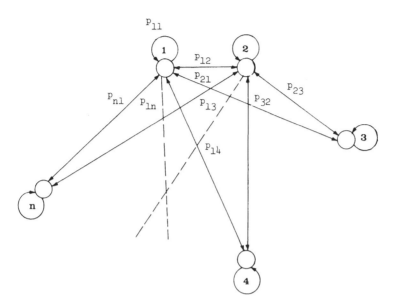

Figure II.4: A Markov Transition Matrix

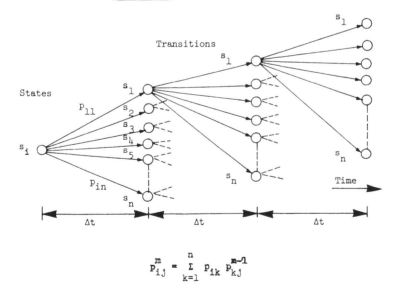

$$p_{ij}^m = \sum_{k=1}^{n} p_{ik}\, p_{kj}^{m-1}$$

Figure II.5: m-Stages Transition Probabilities

The transition probabilities in k steps are given by raising the matrix $P = [P_{ij}]$ to the kth power. (See Figure II.5).

We will now consider continuous Markov processes by letting the time intervals Δt become very samll and be denoted by "dt". The transition probability in dt will then be given by:

$$p_{ij}^{dt} = q_{ij}dt + 0(dt) \quad i \neq j$$

where $0(dt)$ are terms tending towards zero faster than dt. Thus:

$$\frac{0(dt)}{dt} \to 0 \quad \text{as} \quad dt \to 0$$

In the modeling of economic and business processes we are usually given or assume the infinitesimal transition probabilities q_{ij}. Alternatively, a probability model can be constructed and the probabilities q_{ij} found by estimation techniques.[25] It is quite evident that since we have a Markov process, the Chapman-Kolmogorov equations hold and therefore rewriting:

$$P_{ij}(t + dt) = p_{ij}^{t+dt}$$

we obtain:

$$P_{ij}(t + dt) = \sum_{k=1}^{n} p_{ik}(dt) \, p_{kj}(t)$$

Replacing $p_{ik}(dt)$ by $(q_{ik})dt + 0(dt)$:

$$P_{ij}(t + dt) = \sum_{k=1}^{n} [q_{ik}dt + 0(dt)]p_{kj}(t)$$

$$P_{ij}(t + dt) = q_{ii}(dt) + \sum_{k \neq i} q_{ik} \, p_{kj}(t)dt$$

$$= (1 - Q_i dt) \, p_{ij}(t) + dt \sum_{k \neq i} q_{ik} p_{kj}(t)$$

where q_{ii} the probability of remaining in state i is given by $1 - Q_i dt$ with

$$Q_i = \sum_{k \neq i} q_{ik}$$

Transposing $p_{ij}(t)$ and dividing by dt, we finally obtain Kolmogorov's homogeneous (differential-difference) equation;

$$\frac{dp_{ij}(t)}{dt} = -Q_i p_{ij}(t) + \sum_{k \neq i} q_{ik} p_{kj}(t)$$

where $dp_{ij}(t)/dt$ is the time derivative of the probability $p_{ij}(t)$ at time t. The stationary probabilities are found by letting:

$$dp_{ij}(t)/dt = 0$$

or

$$-Q_i p_{ij} + \sum_{k \neq i} q_{ik} p_{kj} = 0$$

where p_{ij} are the limit probabilities described by a system of difference equations. Finally, when the probabilities q_{ij} may be a function of time t, we obtain a non-homogeneous Kolmogorov equation;

$$\frac{dp_{ij}(t)}{dt} = -Q_i(t) \, p_{ij}(t) + \sum_{k \neq i} q_{ik}(t) \, p_{kj}(t)$$

which is a system of time-variant linear differential equations.

The Kolmogorov differential-difference equations describe the evolution in time of probability distributions (as does the Fokker-Plank equation). These distributions are discrete; that is, the set of feasible states a random variable may take is discrete rather than continuous. We shall show in Chapter V that it is possible to approximate discrete states by continuous ones. This will involve finding the approximate Fokker-Plank equation of a given Kolmogorov equation. This is called a diffusion approximation.

Examples of Markov processes will be considered in Section II.5. Specifically, we shall show how to construct stochastic processes based on hypotheses about transition probabilities. Applications to queueing, advertising and discounting will then be considered.

(5) The Poisson Process

The Poisson process, a special case of Markov processes, assumes (as the Wiener-Levy process) independent and identically distributed increments. This process is of considerable importance in management applications to queueing theory. We shall obtain below the probability distribution of the process by an application of the foregoing section. Specifically, assume that we are at time t+dt is a given state n and denote by $p_n(t+dt)$ the probability distribution of this event. This state may be reached if (1) we are in state n-1 at time t and there is a transition to state n with probability λdt, (2) if we are already in state n at t and no transition occurs. This last event occurs with probability $1-\lambda dt$. The corresponding Kolmogorov homogeneous equation is then;

$$\frac{dp_n(t)}{dt} = -\lambda p_n(t) + \lambda p_{n-1}(t) \qquad n > 0$$

And, at the boundary n = 0,

$$\frac{dp_n(t)}{dt} = -\lambda p_0(t)$$

A solution for $p_n(t)$ can be easily shown to be (see Chapter V)

$$p_n(t) = \frac{(\lambda t)^n e^{-t}}{n!}$$

$$n = 0, 1, 2, \ldots$$

where λ is called the process rate.

(6) Stochastic Integrals and Stochastic Differential Equations

For a certain class of problems, it is convenient to represent the evolution of stochastic processes not as an evolution of probability distributions (as we have done so far), but as an evolution of differential (or difference) equations with random components. Such equations are called stochastic differential (or difference) equations and involve derivatives and integrals over random functions. These derivatives and integrals introduce some quantitative and conceptual difficulties related to the definition of a stochastic calculus. In appendix II.2 an introduction to a mean square calculus as well as a quantitative definition of stochastic integrals and stochastic differential equations is given. Below, we consider some intuitive notions which lead to stochastic integrals and stochastic differential equations.

Consider again the random walk model in pages 90-92 and denote by x_t the position of the point on the line at time t. This is a random function whose realization can be modeled by the stochastic difference equation;

$$x_{t+1} = x_t + \xi_t \qquad x_0 \text{ given}$$
$$t = 0, 1, 2, 3, \ldots$$

where ξ_t denotes a random disturbance at time t. In the example on page 90, we assumed such a disturbance to be given by $\xi_t = \Delta P$ with probability p and $\xi_t = -\Delta P$ with probability 1-p. Moreover, we may consider different disturbances. Specifically, ξ_t may be a Wiener-Levy process, a Poisson process or some other stochastic process. Further, the transition from x_t to x_{t+1} may be given by a linear or by non-linear equations of the form:

or
$$x_{t+1} = A_t x_t + B_t \xi_t$$
$$x_{t+1} = F(x_t, \xi_t)$$
$$x_{t+1} = F(x_t) + G(x_t)\xi_t$$

The first equation is called a stochastic linear difference equation while the latter two equations are called non-linear stochastic difference equations.

To define continuous time, continuous state, stochastic processes we consider now time intervals of length Δt. Of course the case $\Delta t \equiv 1$ corresponds to the stochastic difference equations above. Further, we replace x_t by $x(t)$ and define the difference operator $\Delta x(t)$;
$$\Delta x(t) = x(t+\Delta t) - x(t)$$
The disturbance ξ_t is replaced by $\xi(t)$ and is inserted in the time intervals $[t, t+\Delta t]$. To simplify our presentation, we shall also assume that $x(t)$ and $\xi(t)$ are given by step functions. Specifically, the disturbance $\xi(t)$ in the time interval $[t, t+\Delta t]$ is given by an increment $\Delta\beta(t)$ $(= \beta(t+\Delta t) - \beta(t))$ where $\beta(t)$ will be assumed throughout the book to be a Wiener-Levy process. Therefore $\Delta\beta(t)$ is an independent increment process, as discussed.

Considering the additive disturbance non-linear stochastic difference equation, re-expressed in terms of Δt increments, we obtain,
$$\Delta x(t) = F(x(t), t)\Delta t + G(x(t), t)\Delta\beta(t)$$
We divide both sides of the equation by Δt;
$$\frac{\Delta x(t)}{\Delta t} = F(x(t), t) + G(x(t), t) \frac{\Delta\beta(t)}{\Delta t}$$

and let the time interval Δt become infinitisimally small. Then, assuming mean-square differentiability of $x(t)$ (see Appendix II.2)

$$\lim_{\Delta t \to 0} \frac{\Delta x(t)}{\Delta t} = \frac{dx(t)}{dt}$$

and if $\beta(t)$ is a Wiener-Levy process,

$$\xi(t) \sim \lim_{\Delta t \to 0} \frac{\Delta \beta}{\Delta t} = \frac{d\beta}{dt}$$

where $\xi(t)$ is called a White-noise Gaussian process. This is a zero-mean, normal and uncorrelated random function. That is,

$$E[\xi(t)] = 0$$
$$E[\xi(t)\xi(\tau)] = \delta_D(t-\tau)\sigma^2(x,t)$$

where $\delta_D(t-\tau)$ - called the Dirac **Delta** function, is an impulse function defined for arbitrary small ε by the integrals:

$$\int_{-\infty}^{\infty} \delta_D(t-\tau)dt = 1, \quad \lim_{\varepsilon \to 0} \int_{\tau-|\varepsilon|}^{\tau+|\varepsilon|} \delta_D(t-\tau)dt = 1$$

Thus, $\delta(t-\tau) = 1$ in an ε neighborhood of zero (i.e. at $t = \tau$), and $\delta(t-\tau) = 0$ elsewhere. Finally, $\sigma^2(x,t)$ is an instantaneous variance of the process. When we consider the limit ($\Delta t \to 0$) a stochastic differential equation is obtained;

$$\frac{dx(t)}{dt} = F(x(t), t) + G(x(t), t)\xi(t)$$
$$x(t_0) = x^0 \text{ given}$$

This equation is meaningful, however, in so far as its solution;

$$x(t) - x(t_0) = \int_{t_0}^{t} F(x(t),t)dt + \int_{t} G(x(t),t)d\beta(t)$$

is meaningful. This solution consists of two integrals. The first integral is well defined in standard calculus. The second integral is called a stochastic integral and its definition is difficult because of the unbounded variation of the Wiener-Levy process $\beta(t)$. There are however two definitions of such an integral - Itô and Stratonovich (see Appendix II.2 for limiting conditions on $F(x(t), t)$, $G(x(t), t)$ and $\sigma^2(x,t)$). Partition of the time interval $[t, t_0]$ into N steps of length $t_{j+1}^\rho - t_j^\rho$, $j = 0, 1, \ldots, N-1$ where $\rho = \max_j(t_{j+1} - t_j)$ and $t_0 = t_0$, $t = t_N$ leads to the following definitions of stochastic integrals;[26]

The Itô Stochastic integral $\int$, under suitable restrictions on the continuity and boundedness of $G(x(t), t)$ and $\sigma^2(x(t), t)$, is defined as the limit in mean of

$$\int_t^\rho G(x(t),t)d\beta(t) = \lim_{\rho \to 0} \sum_{j=1}^{N-1} G(x(t_j),t_j)[\beta(t_{j+1})-\beta(t_j)]$$

The Stratonovich stochastic integral $\oint$, under suitable restrictions on the continuity and boundedness of $G(x(t), t)$ and $\sigma^2(x,t)$ is defined as the limit in mean

$$\oint G(x(t),t)d\beta(t) = \lim_{\rho \to 0} \sum_{j=1}^{N-1} G(\frac{x(t_j)+x(t_{j+1})}{2},t_j)[\beta(t_{j+1})-\beta(t_j)]$$

The Itô and Stratonovich stochastic integrals are not the same, however. If G is a function of β it has been shown by Stratonovich that they are related with probability one by;

$$\oint_t G(\beta(t),t)d\beta(t) = \int_t G(\beta(t),t)d\beta(t) +$$

$$+ \frac{1}{2}\int_t \frac{\partial G(\beta(t),t)}{\partial \beta} \cdot \sigma^2(x(t),t)d\beta(t)$$

In this book we shall use Itô's stochastic calculus and formally write an Itô stochastic differential equation as:

$$dx(t) = F(x(t),t)dt + G(x(t),t)d\beta(t)$$

It will be then understood that a solution exists if the stochastic integrals above exist. That is, the limit in mean of the area of step functions with infinitisimally small step lengths exists. A solution to Itô's stochastic differential equation by "stochastic integration" provides a solution in terms of random functions. A different but complementary solution consists in determining the evolution in time of the probability distributions $p(x,t)$ of the stochastic process $\{x(t); t \geq 0\}$. Remembering that Itô's stochastic differential equation is a Markov process, and assuming existence and continuity of the partial derivatives,

$$\frac{\partial p}{\partial t}, \frac{\partial p}{\partial x}, \frac{\partial^2 p}{\partial x^2}$$

it can be shown that $p(x,t)$ is given by the solution of a Fokker-Plank (diffusion) equation;

$$\frac{\partial p(x,t)}{\partial t} = -\frac{\partial}{\partial x}[F(x,t)p(x,t)] + \frac{1}{2}\frac{\partial^2}{\partial x^2}[G^2(x,t)\sigma^2(x,t)p(x,t)]$$

with initial conditions $p(x,t_0)$ given. A solution to this equation as indicated in Section II.4(2) and II.4(3) is difficult. Special cases with specific assumptions concerning F, G and σ^2 may be resolved, however. In Section II.4(3) we considered for example, the special cases of Brownian motion (F = 0, G = 1, $\sigma^2(x,t) = 1$).

The modelisation of stochastic differential (or difference) equations provides the quantitative framework required to describe the evolution of processes under uncertainty. In this respect, this section is a counterpart to Sections II.2 and II.3 which dealt with deterministic processes. Below we consider specific management examples which will be investigated in greater detail in Chapters III and V when problems of estimation and stochastic control (i.e. decision making in uncertain dynamic systems) will be defined and resolved.

II.5 Applications

Example II.6: Time Series

The record of a moving particle or a random variable as it progresses in time is a <u>time series</u>. For example, the record of a stock price, the number of cars registered each year, the demand for gasoline or for a product over time are all instances of time series.

Given one or a set of random variables taking on values discretely or continuously in time, the model describing the probabilistic evolution of these values is the <u>stochastic process</u>. The record of these values is time series. Specifically, if $z_0,\ldots,z_n$ is a record of random variables $x_0,\ldots,x_n$ at times $t_0, t_1,\ldots,t_n$, and if this record includes measurement errors, we write

$$z_i = x_i + \eta_i \qquad i = 0, 1, 2, \ldots, n$$

where η_i is a random disturbance. The evolution of x_i can be modeled, for example, by the stochastic difference equation

$$i = 1, 2, 3, \ldots, n$$
$$x_{i+1} = f\{x_i, \xi_i\}$$
$$x_0 \text{ given}$$

where ξ_i is a random disturbance used to describe the uncertainty in the evolution of x_i.

A continuous-time equivalent formulation to this stochastic process is given by

$$\frac{dx(t)}{dt} = f(x(t), \xi(t))$$
$$z(t) = x(t) + \eta(t)$$

Such models will be used repeatedly to describe the random and continuous time movement of variables such as; price indices, demand for a product, goodwill, etc.

Example II.7: Exponential Smoothing

We return to example II.2 and consider the difference equation

$$D_t = (1-\delta)D_{t-1} + \delta d_t$$

A solution for D_t (by iteration) yields

$$D_t = \delta d_t + \delta(1-\delta)d_{t-1} + \delta(1-\delta)^2 d_{t-2}$$
$$+ \ldots + \delta(1-\delta)^{k-1} d_{t-k+1} + (1-\delta)^k d_{t-k}$$

When k tends to infinity

$$D_t = \delta \sum_{k=0}^{\infty} (1-\delta)^k d_{t-k}$$

Now assume that d_t are uncorrelated and independently distributed random variables with zero mean, and constant variance.

$$E(d_t) = 0, \quad var(d_t) = \sigma^2$$

Then

$$E(D_t) = 0 \text{ and}$$
$$var(D_t) = \delta^2 \sum_{k=0}^{\infty} (1-\delta)^{2k} \sigma^2 = \frac{\delta \sigma^2}{2-\delta}$$

Also, the covariance at two instants of time t and $t+\tau$ is:

$$cov[D_t, D_{t+\tau}] = \delta^2 \sum_{k=0}^{\infty} (1-\delta)^{\tau+2k} \sigma^2 = \frac{\delta(1-\delta)^{\tau}}{2-\delta} \sigma^2$$

The correlation function is thus

$$r_{\tau} = \frac{cov(D_t, D_{t+\tau})}{\sqrt{var(D_t)var(D_{t+\tau})}} = (1-\delta)^{\tau}$$

$$\tau = 0, 1, 2, \ldots$$

The stochastic process of D_t thus defined is strictly stationary. That is, the distribution is time invariant, and the covariance (as well as the correlation) is a function of the time difference.

If we consider the continuous time version of the exponential smoothing equation, we have now a linear stochastic differential equation

$$\frac{dD(t)}{dt} = -\delta D(t) + \delta \varepsilon(t)$$

where $\varepsilon(t)$ replaces d_t. Using the results of section II.4(6), the evolution of the probability distribution of $D(t)$ is given by the Fokker-Plank diffusion equation;

$$\frac{\partial p}{\partial t} = - \frac{\delta \partial}{\partial D}[D(t)p(D,t)] + \frac{\delta}{2} \sigma^2 \frac{\partial^2 p(D,t)}{\partial D^2}$$

This particular process is known as the Ornstein-Uhlenbeck process. Without going through the details of a solution it can be verified that a solution yields the normal probability distribution below;

$$p(D,t|D_0)) = \frac{1}{\sqrt{2\pi v^2(t)}} \exp\left\{-\frac{[D - m(t)]^2}{2v(t)}\right\}$$

with

$$m(t) = D_0 \exp(-\delta t)$$
$$v(t) = 2\sigma^2(1 - e^{-2\delta t})$$

at the initial time $D_0 = 0$, we obtain $m(t) = 0$. When time goes to infinity, we obtain

$$m(t) = 0 \quad \text{and} \quad v(t) = 2\sigma^2$$

Example II.8: Autoregressive Model

Consider the difference equation

$$x_t = ax_{t-1} + \varepsilon_t \qquad t = \ldots -1, 0, 1, 2, \ldots$$

where a is a constant, and assume that ε_t is a sequence of uncorrelated random variables identically distributed with a zero mean and constant variance σ^2. A solution for x_t yields

$$x_t = \sum_{i=0}^{\infty} a^i \varepsilon_{t-i}$$

and

$$E(x_t) = 0$$
$$\text{var}(x_t) = \left(\sum_{i=0}^{t-1} a^2\right)\sigma^2 = \left(\frac{1 - a^{2t}}{1 - a^2}\right)\sigma^2$$

Also, the covariance is;

$$\text{cov}(x_t, x_{t+\tau}) = E\{(\sum_{i=0}^{t+\tau-1} a^i \varepsilon_{t+\tau-i})(\sum_{j=0}^{t-1} a^j \varepsilon_{t-j})$$

$$= (\sum_{i=0}^{t-1} a^i a^{i+\tau})\sigma^2 = (\frac{1-a^{2t}}{1-a^2})a^\tau \sigma^2$$

while the correlation is;

$$r_\tau = \frac{\text{cov}(x_t, x_{t+\tau})}{\sqrt{\text{var}(x_t)\text{var}(x_{t+\tau})}} = \frac{(1-a^{2t})a^\tau}{\sqrt{(1-a^{2t})(1-a^{2(t+2\tau)})}}$$

A time continuous version of the autoregressive model is given by;

$$dx(t)/dt = (a-1)x(t) + \varepsilon(t)$$

which is a stochastic differential equation of the Ornstein-Uhknbeck type, discussed earlier.

Example II.9: Advertising--A Diffusion Model

In this example, we formulate a stochastic process which describes the evolution of the probability distribution of sales as a function of a time-variant advertising strategy, and an exponential forgetting rate of past advertising effort.

Assume that advertising expenditures affect the probability of sales and that "forgetting"--reflecting the decline of sales in the absence of promotions and under relatively stable market conditions--is also probabilistic. Thus, we assume that advertising expenditures affect the probability of sales and that in a small time interval Δt, the probability that sales will increase by one unit is a function of this advertising rate. Similarly, in a time interval Δt, the probability that sales will decrease by one unit is a function of the forgetting rate. Such a process will be described below as a random walk with two reflecting barriers.

Consider, for example, a line taking the values $x = 0, 1, 2, 3,...,M$ where x represents a level of sales and M is the total market potential (see Figure II.6)

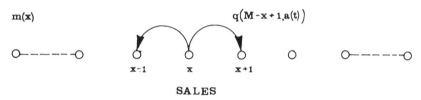

SALES

Figure II.6: The Stochastic Model

Denote by $P(x,t)$ the probability of selling x at time t. At time $t+\Delta t$, the probability of selling x is given by:

$$P(x,t+\Delta t) = P(x+1,t)m(x+1)\Delta t + P(x,t)[1-m(x)\Delta t][1-q(M-x,a(t))\Delta t] + P(x-1,t)[q(M-x+1,a(t))]\Delta t$$

where $m(x)\Delta t$ is the probability that a unit of sales is lost by forgetting. This probability is given as a function m of the aggregate demand x and the forgetting rate m. The probability that a unit sales is generated by an advertising effort $a(t)$ in a time interval Δt is given by the function $q(M-x,a(t))\Delta t$ where $M-x$ denotes the magnitude of a potential and as yet unrealized demand, and $a(t)$ is the advertising rate at time t.

Hypothesize that the forgetting rate and advertising effectiveness are given by;

$$m(x) = mx; \quad q(M-x,a(t)) = qa(t)(M-x)$$

That is, the probability that a sales unit is lost in a small time interval Δt is proportional to the current level of sales x and the forgetting rate m. Similarly, the probability that a sales unit is gained in a time interval dt is proportional to the remaining market potential M-x and to the advertising rate a(t). By varying the advertising rate a(t), we can manipulate the probability of gaining one additional sales unit in the time interval Δt. Inserting these hypotheses into the advertising stochastic process and letting Δt be very small, the process with appropriate boundary restrictions on x reduces to:

$$\frac{dP(x,t)}{dt} = m(x+1)P(x+1,t) - [mx+qa(t)(M-x)]P(x,t) + qa(t)(M-x+1)P(x-1,t) \quad x = 1, 2, \ldots, M-1$$

$$\frac{dP(0,t)}{dt} = mP(1,t) - Mqa(t)P(0,t)$$

$$\frac{dP(M,t)}{dt} = -mMP(M,t) + qa(t)P(M-1,t)$$

This equation describes the probabilistic evolution of sales at time t as a function of the advertising rate a(t) and the forgetting rate m.

Although an anlytical solution for P(x,t) is complicated, an expression for the probability moments of sales at time t, can be found easily.

A mean-variance evolution for the probability distribution of demand to be proved in Chapter V is given by [27]

$$ds(t)/dt = Mqa(t) - (m+qa(t))s(t) \quad s(0) = s^0$$

and

$$dv(t)/dt = Mqa(t) + (m-qa(t))s(t) - (m+qa(t))2v(t)$$

$$v(0) = 0$$

where s(t) is the mean demand at time t and v(t) is the variance.

If the advertising rate is constant, $a(t) = a$, integration of $ds(t)/dt$ and $dv(t)/dt$ yields

$$s(t) = \frac{mqa}{qa+m}(1 - e^{-(qa+m)t/M}) + s^0 e^{-(qa+m)t/M}$$

$$v(t) = s(t)(1-s(t)/M) - (s^0/M)(M-s^0)e^{-2(qa+m)t/M}$$

At the limit $t \to \infty$

$$s_\infty = Mqa/(qa+m)$$
$$v_\infty = s_\infty(1-s_\infty/M)$$

In other words, at the limit, the market share for a constant advertising rate a is given by $qa/[qa+m]$, while the variance of sales per unit of the market potential M is given by $(qa)(m)/[qa+m]^2$.

Example II.10: Advertising, Goodwill and Uncertainty

Here we pursue example II.3 by letting the goodwill induced by an advertising policy be defined by a stochastic process. The model we construct consists again in hypothesizing a probabilistic effect of advertising on goodwill and finding the appropriate transition probabilities.

Assume that goodwill for a product at time t is described by a stochastic process $\{x(t); t \geq 0\}$. This goodwill is a random variable taking integer values on half the line $x = 0, 1, 2,\ldots$. Denote by $P(x,t)$ the probability that the goodwill is x at time t. At time $t+\Delta t$, transitions to a state of goodwill x can occur in three essential cases by **"forgetting"**, **"recall"**, by advertising and no "forgetting" and no "recall".

Hypothesize, as in Example II.9, that

$$m(x,t) = mx$$

$$q(M-x,a(t)) = q(a(t))$$

where $mx\Delta t$ is the probability of losing one unit of goodwill to forgetting, while $q(a(t))\Delta t$ is a function of advertising expenditures denoting the probability of increasing goodwill by one unit in a time interval Δt. Pooling the probability effects of forgetting and advertising on goodwill, and assuming their statistical independence, we obtain a stochastic process with a reflecting barrier at $x = 0$. As in example II.9 we obtain the stochastic process

$$\frac{dP(x,t)}{dt} = -[mx + q(a(t))]P(x,t) + m(x+1)P(x+1,t) + q(a(t))P(x-1,t)$$

and the reflecting barrier

$$\frac{dP(0,t)}{dt} = -q(a(t))P(0,t) + mP(1,t)$$

There are, however, several important differences between this and the model in example II.9. In example II.9 the market potential was assumed to be finite, while goodwill may be infinite here (albeit with an extremely small probability). Further, while in example II.9 advertising effectiveness was proportionate to the remaining market potential, it is assumed here to be independent of such a market. In both cases, however, sales reflecting a state of goodwill can be influenced probabilistically by advertising. It is worthwhile to point out at this time that the mean-variance evolutions are given by:

$$ds(t)/dt = q(a(t)) - ms(t)$$

$$s(0) = s^0$$

$$dv(t)/dt = [q(a(t))+m]s(t) - 2mv(t)$$

$$v(0) = 0$$

This will be proved in Chapter V.

Example II.11: A stochastic process of machine's maintenance and deterioration

We pursue example II.5 and include the probabilistic effects of maintenance and deterioration in computing a machine's value. Now we assume that the salvage value of the machine at time t is a stochastic process $\{x(t); t \geq 0\}$ where $P(x,t)$ describes the time-variant probability distribution of the salvage value. Let the range of x be $\{0, 1, 2,...\}$ and suppose that at time $t+\Delta t$, the probability that the salvage value is $x(t+\Delta t)$ is given by the following transitions:

$[a(t)+b(t)x(t)]\Delta t$ = the probability that the machine deteriorates by one unit in the time interval $[t+t+\Delta t]$. This probability is a function of $a(t)$ - the obsolescence rate and $b(t)$ - the depreciation rate which is proportional to the value of the machine at time t, $x(t)$.

$f(t)m(t)\Delta t$ = the probability that the machine appreciates in value by one unit through maintenance.

These transition probabilities describe a random walk. Movements increasing the salvage value of the machine are controlled by maintenance expenditures, while movements decreasing the salvage value are due to deterioration and obsolescence. Without difficulty, we can show that this random walk model gives rise to the following differential-difference equation:

$$\frac{dP(x,t)}{dt} = -(fm+a+bx)P(x,t) + [a+b(x+1)]P(x+1,t) + fmP(x-1,t) \qquad x = 1, 2,...$$

with boundary condition

$$\frac{dP(0,t)}{dt} = (a+b)P(1,t) - fmP(0,t)$$

and initial condition

$$P(x = K, 0) = 1$$

where a, b, f and m are time variant.

A mean-variance evolution of the salvage value, dropping the time arguments is given by; (see example V, in Chapter V).[28]

$$ds/dt = -a + fm + 2bs + P(0,t)a$$
$$s(0) = K$$
$$dw/dt = a + fm + [-a + fm + 2b + P(0,t)a]s - 6bs^2 - 4bw - P(0,t)a$$
$$w(0) = 0$$

where s(t) is the mean salvage value at time t, w(t) is the variance, and P(0,t) is an unknown probability of zero-salvage value at time t. If a machine is retired long before it reaches a state of zero-salvage value, then $P(0,t) \approx 0$ and therefore a mean-variance evolution of the salvage value can be described by the two differential equations above.

Example II.12

Queueing theory is concerned with "waiting lines". For example, communication traffic, telephoning, transportation traffic on highways, queueing for service in supermarkets, airline offices, post offices, inventories, production processes, epidemic processes, population growth, etc. can be thought of as involving waiting lines and can be interpreted as instances of queueing models. Below, we describe a simple birth-death process (which is important in queueing theory) (see Figure II.7) as a random walk model.

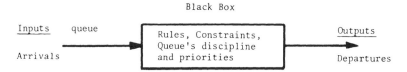

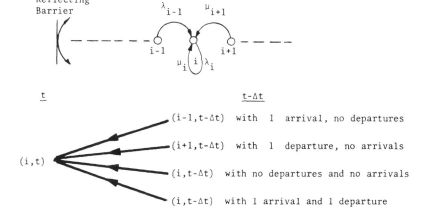

Figure II.7: A Simple Queueing Model

Consider the line, and assume that each position on the line is the number of units (or the number of persons) in the queueing system. Since the number of units (persons) cannot be negative, we have a left-handed reflecting barrier at x = 0. Say that at a given time t, we are in a position i and denote by P(i,t) the probability of being at i at time t. The exhaustive possibilities for our being in i at t are given in Figure II.7 where Δt is a small time increment. During this small time increment, the probability that there will be one arrival is given by $\lambda_i \Delta t$, while the probability that there will be a departure is given by $\mu_i \Delta t$, where λ_i and μ_i are functions of the state i. Thus the probability of having i units at time t is a Markov process as given in section II.4 (4) and for Δt small,

$$|j-i| \leq 1 \quad \text{and}$$

$$\frac{dP(i,t)}{dt} = -(\lambda_i + \mu_i)P(i,t) + \lambda_{i-1}P(i-1,t) + \mu_{i+1}P(i+1,t)$$

Since i cannot be negative (i.e., it is a left-handed reflecting barrier), at i = 0) we obtain:

$$\frac{dP(0,t)}{dt} = -\lambda_0 P(0,t) + \mu_1 P(1,t)$$

These equations describe the evolution of the probability distribution of having i units in the system at time t. If this probability distribution is assumed stationary -- not varying in time -- then $dP(i,t)/dt = 0$ and

$$0 = -(\lambda_i + \mu_i)P(i) + \lambda_{i-1}P(i-1) + \mu_{i+1}P(i+1)$$

$$0 = -\lambda_0 P(0) + \mu_1 P(1)$$

These are simple difference equations whose solution is straightforward. At the initial condition i = 0, and for single server queueing systems

$(\lambda_i = \lambda, \mu_i = \mu)$, thus, solution yields

$$P(i) = (1-\lambda/\mu)(\lambda/\mu)^i$$

which is a geometric probability distribution for i. The mean of this distribution is

$$E(i) = [\lambda/\mu]/[1-\lambda/\mu]$$

Since at any one time, only one "unit" is being served, the remaining units form a queue whose expected length is L_q:

$$L_q = \sum_{i=1}^{\infty} (i-1)P(i) = \lambda^2/\mu(\mu-\lambda)$$

The solution we have obtained is of course for the limit (t = infinity) probability distribution of P(i,t). A direct solution of P(i,t) is more complicated, especially when λ_i and μ_i - the arrival and service rates - are time variant. These cases will be pursued in Chapter V.

II.6 Discounting

(1) Probabilistic-Discount Rates

The importance of discounting indicated repeatedly in Chapter I and this chapter requires that we give it further attention. In this section, we shall elucidate some of the issues associated with the choice of a particular discount rate, distinguish between short and long term discount rates, and provide an empirical method for estimating consumers' discount rate. In section II.2 we pointed out an analogy between time and statistical sampling. The essential similarity between the future and a statistical population is that both are unknown and for both, statistical inference procedures are used. Furthermore, in Chapter I, section I.3 we pointed out the human need to immobilize the flow of time (i.e. seek the fixation of time). This allows a simultaneous comparison of events in time. Both factors are reflected in the use of discounting rates. To compare two sums of money at two different instants of time, it is necessary that each of these sums be transformed into cash equivalents at similar instants of time. The future being essentially unknown the valuation of say, future returns is at best probabilistic. That is, the discount rate expressing an attitude towards future returns also expresses an attitude towards the uncertainty of these returns. In this sense, the discount rate expresses simultaneously a measure of time and risk preferences. Firms, consumers, managers, stockholders etc. exhibit different attitudes towards time and risk which is reflected in different discount rates. What is the appropriate discount rate? and what are the implications of a specific discount rate? To comprehend these questions, a probabilistic framework for the discounting process can be useful.

Specifically, consider an investor estimating the present value $x(t)$ of a future return of \$S at time t. The investor's attitude towards the future -- i.e. his time preference -- is probabilistic, and will be assumed to be a stochastic process. The problem here does not lie in the choice of the discount rate, but rather in how the investor values returns if they are in the distant future. Also, to what extent do delays in the time and the size of returns affect present valuation of the investor? These are questions which we shall attempt to answer by considering a population of investors whose collective behavior can be characterized by the stochastic process constructed below.

Assume that $x(t)$ is a discrete state random function of time expressing the value now of \$S at time t. ($x(t) = 0, 1, \ldots, S$). As time t changes so does the value $x(t)$. Now suppose that $x(t)$

is modeled by a stochastic process described in Figure II.8. That
is, the probability P(x, t+Δt), of a value now of $S at t+ t

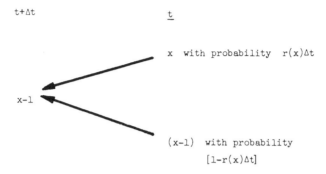

Figure II.8: A Stochastic Process of Discounting

is conditional upon the value at time t and is a function of
r(x,t)Δt -- interpreted as the conditional probability of losing one
dollar in present value by delaying the time of return of $S from t
to t+Δt. This probability is assumed to be a function of the size
of the present value $x(t)$ of the return S at time t. Using the
transition probabilities in Figure II.8 we construct a stochastic
discounting process:

$$P(x, t+\Delta t) = P(x+1, t)r(x+1, t)\Delta t + P(x,t)[1-r(x,t)\Delta t]$$

$$P(0, t+\Delta t) = P(1,t)r(1,t)\Delta t;$$

$$P(x = S, 0) = 1$$

At the limit, when $\Delta t \to 0$, we obtain:

$P(x = S, 0) = 1$

$\dfrac{dP(x,t)}{dt} = P(x+1, t) r(x+1, t) - P(x,t) r(x,t)$

$\dfrac{dP(0,t)}{dt} = P(1,t) r(1,t)$

This is a discrete random walk model of present valuation, and provides a probabilistic interpretation of the discounting process. The process of discounting, in turn, is expressed by the numerical values and functional form of the transition probabilities. For simplicity, we hypothesize a <u>linear discounting</u> process, stating that:

$r(x,t) dt = rx dt$

Or, the probability of losing $1 in present valuation by delaying the payment of $S by "dt" is proportional to $x(t)$. Using this hypothesis yields a solution for $P(x,t)$ which will be proved in Chapter V.

$P(x,t) = \binom{S}{x} e^{-rtx} [1 - e^{-rt}]^{S-x}$

This is a binomial probability distribution whose mean and variance are given by $m(t)$ and $v(t)$ respectively;

$m(t) = S e^{-rt}$

$u(t) = S e^{-rt} (1 - e^{-rt})$

The mean $m(t)$ is also recognized at once as the continuous discounting mechanism. This model was derived by making specific assumptions concerning the discounting processes. To what extent are these assumptions correct? The validity of a discounting process is entirely a function of the assumptions implicit in the process. In our case, the assumptions are: (1) The process for comparing two sums of money is timeless, i.e. it is repeated from instant to instant irrespective of the state we find ourselves in and irrespective of time. (2) Given x at t, the probability that x depreciates by $1 in a time interval Δt is proportional to x and to r - the discount rate. This assumption does not take into account the utility of money.

If we add to these two assumptions the fact that the discounting process is a random walk model, we can categorically state that the use of discounting mechanisms as given above is valid for social and economic problems involving small variations in the environment, small time spans and little uncertainty concerning the occurrence of future events. The discount rate r is therefore a short term discount rate. Mechanisms for long term discount rates cannot be constructed as we have done here since the implicit assumptions of the random walk model (timeliness of the jumping process) would probably be violated.

The model we constructed for probabilistic present valuation can of course be extended in several directions. Specifically, assume an independent stream of payment returns $S_1, S_2,...,S_n$ at times $t_1, t_2,...,t_n$. The present value of these payments is a random variable $\tilde{x}$, where

$$\tilde{x} = \sum_{i=1}^{n} \tilde{x}_i$$

with
$$P(x_i, t_i) = \binom{S_i}{x_i} e^{-rt_i x_i} [1 - e^{-rt_i}]^{S_i - x_i}$$

In other words, the present value x is a sum of random variables independently distributed as binomial probability distributions. The probability distribution of x is not binomial, however, except if $S_i = S$ for all $i = 1,\ldots,m$. To compute this distribution, we use generating function techniques to be introduced in Chapter V.

In deterministic present valuation, the mean $m(t)$ **equals** zero only when time t tends to infinity. In our probabilistic discounting process, we note that the probability that \$S at t has zero present value is given by:

$$P(0,t) = (1 - e^{-rt})^S$$

We shall show in Chapter V that this distribution has a mean m_0 approximately given by:

$$m_0 = (\ln S/r^2)$$

For discounting long run returns, we can proceed in two different directions: (1) maintain the assumptions of random walk models and hypothesize a non-linear function $r(x,t)$ expressing now the term structure of interest rates;[30] (2) restrict the range over which a given amount of money, or the present value of a resource can be discounted. The latter assumption would lead to an absorbing barrier in our discounting process.

The "random walk discounting process" considered above provides an approach to probabilistic valuation. There are other approaches, however. Specifically, consider a randomization of the deterministic discounting process. Then

$$\frac{dx}{dt} = -\tilde{r}x(t) \qquad x(0) = S$$

where $\tilde{r}$ - the discount rate - is a random variable. Let $\tilde{r} = r - \xi(t)$ where $\xi(t)$ is a White Gaussian process with variance $2b$. Then, the stochastic differential equation;

$$\frac{dx}{dt} = -rx(t) + x(t)\xi(t)$$

also describes a present valuation process with probabilistic discounting. This equation has a solution which will be shown to be different from that of the "random-walk discounting process."

We note (see section II.4.(6)) that the Fokker-Plank diffusion equation is given by:

$$\frac{\partial f}{\partial t} = r\frac{\partial}{\partial x} xf + b \frac{\partial^2}{\partial x} (x^2 f)$$

A solution of this equation in Chapter V will specifically show that $x(t)$ has a log-normal probability distribution

$$f(x,t|S) = \frac{1}{2x\sqrt{\pi b}} \exp\{-\frac{[\ln x/S - rt]^2}{4bt}\}$$

This is of course different than the binomial process found earlier.

(2) The Probability Distribution of Consumers' Discount Rates

We reconsider section I.5.(3) in Chapter I and establish the theoretical probability distribution of consumers' discount rates.

Let us look first at the case of a consumer who faces a choice of buying a new car with cash or of selecting one of a variety of credit plans available to him. His credit decision involves, among other considerations, his subjective discount rate r_c, the market rate which he must pay for credit r_m, the down payment c_0, if any, and the number T and amount of payments c_1 (which include the finance charge). The discounted sum of future payments at the market finance rate is the purchase price K. The present value of the future payments at the consumer's discount rate is the subjective cost K_1 of the product to the consumer. For consumers who buy on credit, the difference between the purchase price including finance charges and the subjective cost of the credit transaction represents the consumer's surplus involved in all but the marginal credit transaction:

$$K = C_0 + C_1 \sum_{t=0}^{T} (1 + r_m/12)^{-t}$$

$$\Delta = K - C_0 - C_1 \sum_{t=0}^{T} (1 + r_c/12)^{-t}$$

where K = purchase price, dollar amount; C_0 = down payment, dollar amount; C_1 = monthly payment dollar amount; T = **number of payments**; r_d = borrower's discount rate, credit purchasers; r_m = market finance rate; r_c = consumers discount rate, all potential purchasers; Δ = consumers surplus, dollar amount expressing the residual value to the consumer when using credit plan.

If the surplus is positive, the consumer will purchase on credit. The condition for a credit transaction is therefore $\Delta > 0$, and $r_c \geq r_m$. By definition, we let r_d be the borrowers discount rate to be equal to r_c conditional upon $r_c \geq r_m$. Then

$$\sum_{t=0}^{T} (1 + r_d/12)^{-t} \leq \sum_{t=0}^{T} (1 + r_m/12)^{-t}$$

This establishes the condition for a credit transaction given a market rate. Now assume that the discount rate is to be empirically estimated. Specifically, we shall consider the case of credit financing in "buy now pay later" plans and find the probability distribution $f(r_c)$ of consumers' discount rate r_c.

Assume that the number of credit transactions with T payments at a market rate r_m is given by $D(r_m,T)$. We postulate this demand function to be proportional to the expected consumers' surplus, that is:[31]

$$D(r_m,t) \alpha \int_{r_m}^{\infty} \int_0^T e^{-r_c T} f(r_c) dT dr_c = \int_{r_m}^{\infty} \frac{1-e^{-r_c T}}{r_c} f(r_c) dr_c$$

where integration is taken for r_c greater than r_m. Let $G(T)$ be the propportionality constant. Then,

$$D(r_m,T) = \frac{1}{G(T)} \int_{r_m}^{\infty} \frac{1-e^{-r_c T}}{r_c} f(r_c) dr_c$$

Taking a partial derivative of $D(r_m,T)$ with respect to r_m, the market rate, we obtain:

$$f(r_c) = -\frac{\partial D}{\partial r_c} G(T) / \left(\frac{1-e^{-r_c T}}{r_c}\right)$$

This is a probability function proportional to the marginal change in the demand for credit and inversely proportional to the credit cost of a dollar payment over T periods, both at the market rate r_m. When T, the number of payments is infinite, G is not a function of T and we obtain

$$f(r_c) = -\frac{\partial D}{\partial r_c} G r_c \quad \text{and} \quad \int_0^{\infty} f(r_c) dr_c = 1$$

With these equations we solve for $G(T)$ the proportionality constant in the finite payment case and obtain;

$$f(r_c) = \frac{r_c(\partial D/\partial r_c)/(1-e^{-r_c T})}{\int_0^{\infty} r_c(\partial D/\partial r_c)/(1-e^{-r_c T}) dr_c}$$

where $f(r_c)$ is the probability distribution of a consumer's discount rate when the number of payments T is finite. When T is infinite, $f(r_c)$ reduces to;

$$f(r_c) = \frac{r_c \partial D/\partial r_c}{\int_0^{\infty} r_c \partial D/\partial r_c dr_c}$$

Therefore, given the demand for credit $D(r_m,T)$ as a function of the market rate r_m, an empirical probability distribution of a consumer's rate can be found. Assume that the demand function is of the form:

$$D(r_m) = \bar{D} \, e^{-ar_m^n} \qquad \bar{D}, a, n > 0$$

We can then show that when T is infinite, the probability distribution of r_c (dropping the subscript c) is given by:[32]

$$f(r) = \frac{na^{(1+1/n)} r^n e^{-ar^n}}{\Gamma(1+1/n)}$$

where Γ is the gamma function, defined by

$$\Gamma(x) = \int_0^\infty t^{x-1} e^{-t} dt$$

By transformation of variables;

$$f(y) = \frac{y^{1/n} e^{-y}}{\Gamma(1+1/n)}, \quad y = ar^n \quad y > 0$$

which is a standard gamma distribution with mean given by $E\{y\} = 1 + 1/n$. Thus, for $n = 1$ $E\{r\} = \{2/a\}$.

When the number of payments is finite, the gamma probability distribution is no longer appropriate. Another distribtuion is required, for example, if credit transactions require repayment within a finite schedule of T payments. Proceeding as before we find that;

$$f(r) = \frac{ar \, e^{-ar}/(1-e^{-rT})}{\int_0^\infty [ar \, e^{-ar}/(1-e^{-rT})] dr}$$

The integral in the denominator above is a Riemann-Zeta integral.[33] Thus

$$f(r) = \frac{T^2 r \, e^{-ar}}{(1 - e^{-rT}) \sum_{n=0}^\infty \frac{1}{(n+a/T)^2}}$$

Or,

$$f(y) = \frac{y \, e^{-y}}{\gamma^2 (1 - e^{-y/\gamma}) \sum_{n=0}^\infty 1/(n+\gamma)^2}$$

$$y = ar, \quad \gamma = a/T$$

The pth moment is given by[34]

$$E\{y^p\} = \frac{\Gamma(p+1)\xi(p+1,\gamma)}{\gamma^{p+3}\xi(2,\gamma)}$$

Thus the mean is

$$E\{y\} = \frac{\Gamma(2)\xi(3,\gamma)}{\gamma^4\xi(2,\gamma)} \quad \text{with} \quad E(r) = E(y)/a$$

and the variance is

$$\text{var}\{y\} = \frac{\Gamma(3)\xi(4,\gamma)}{\gamma^5\xi(2,\gamma)} - E\{y\}^2$$

or $\text{var}(r) = \text{var}(y)/a^2$. The probability distributions we have obtained provide theoretical probability distributions of consumer's discount rate when the demand for credit is given by $D(r_m,T) = \bar{D}\exp(-ar_m^n)$. Such a demand function needs to be estimated, of course. Empirical evidence considered in the next section will show that such a functional form is indeed acceptable.

Given the probability distribution of consumers' discount rates, it is then possible to calculate the probability of a credit transaction as a function of r_m, the market rate. This distribution is simply given by the tail of the distribution to the right of r_m.

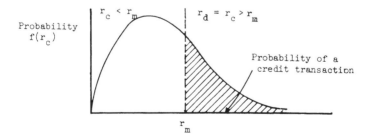

Figure II.9

This probability is clearly given by (see Figure II.9)
$$\int_{r_m}^{\infty} f(r_c)dr_c$$

When r_m increases, the smaller the tail and therefore the smaller the probability of a credit transaction. If we consider a population of borrowers only (those consumers with an r_c to the right of r_m, (i.e., r_d), we note that the probability distribution of r_d is in fact a truncated distribution function of r_m -- the truncation point.

$$\overline{f}(r_d) = \frac{f(r_d)}{\int_{r_m}^{\infty} f(r_c)dr_c}$$

$$r_m \leq r_d < \infty$$

The mean rate of discount is of course

$$E\{r_d\} = \int_{r_m}^{\infty} r_d \overline{f}(r_d)dr_d$$

For the infinite number of payments case, $\overline{f}(r_d)$ is given by:

$$\overline{f}(r_d) = \frac{r_d^n e^{-ar_d^n}}{\int_{r_m}^{\infty} r_d^n e^{-ar_d^n} dr_d}$$

Using again the change of variables $y = ar^n$, $\overline{f}(r_d)$ is given by

$$\overline{f}(y_d) = \frac{y_d^{1/n} e^{-y_d}}{\int_{ar_m^n}^{\infty} t^{1/n} e^{-t} dt}$$

where

$$\int_{ar_m^n}^{\infty} t^{1/n} e^{-t} dt = \Gamma(1 + \frac{1}{n}, ar_m^n)$$

is the incomplete gamma integral and

$$\Gamma(1 + \frac{1}{n}, ar_m^n) = \Gamma(1 + \frac{1}{n})Q(\Psi^2/\nu)$$

$$\nu = 2(1 + \frac{1}{n}); \Psi^2 = 2ar_m^n$$

where $Q(\Psi^2/\nu)$ is the chi-square probability function given by

$$Q(\Psi^2/\nu) = 1 - P(\Psi^2/\nu) = [2^{\nu/2}\Gamma(\nu/2)]^{-1} \int_{\Psi^2}^{\infty} t^{\nu/2-1} e^{-t/2} dt$$

$$0 \leq \Psi^2 < \infty$$

which has been extensively tabulated.[35] $\bar{f}(y_d)$ may therefore be written as:

$$\bar{f}(y_d) = \frac{y_d^{\nu/2-1} e^{-y_d}}{Q(\Psi^2/\nu)\Gamma(\nu/2)}$$

$$\Psi^2 = 2ar_m^n \qquad \nu = 2(1 + \frac{1}{n})$$

The moments of y_d can be computed. Specifically,

$$E\{y_d^z\} = \frac{\int_{ar_m^n}^{\infty} y^{\nu/2+z-1} e^{-y_d} dy}{Q(\Psi^2/\nu)\Gamma(\nu/2)} = \frac{Q(\Psi^2|\nu + 2z)\Gamma(\nu/2 + z)}{Q(\Psi^2|\nu)\Gamma(\nu/2)}$$

The mean is therefore

$$E\{y_d\} = \frac{Q(\Psi^2|\nu+2)(\nu/2)}{Q(\Psi^2|\nu)}$$

while the variance is:

$$\text{var}\{y_d\} = \frac{\{Q(\Psi^2|\nu+4)(\frac{\nu}{2}+1)(\frac{\nu}{2})\}}{Q(\Psi^2|\nu)} - \frac{Q^2(\Psi^2|\nu+2)(\nu/2)^2}{Q^2(\Psi^2|\nu)}$$

The mean and the variance of the borrower's discount rate for the case $n = 1$ is therefore;

$$E\{r_d\} = \frac{1}{a} E\{y_d\}$$

$$\text{var}\{r_d\} = \frac{1}{a^2} \text{var}\{y_d\}$$

For example, if $a = 50$, then we obtain the following means and variances for borrower's rates. (See Table II.5).

r_m	0.10	0.12	0.14	0.16	0.18	0.20
ψ^2	.10	12	14	16	18	20
$Q(\psi^2/4)$	.04043	.01735	.00730	.00302	.00123	.00050
$Q(\psi^2/6)$	.12465	.06197	.02964	.01375	.00623	.00277
$Q(\psi^2/8)$	.26503	.15120	.08177	.04238	.02123	.01034
$E\{y_d\}$	6.16621	7.1435	8.1205	9.1059	10.130	11.08
$E\{r_d\}$	.12332	.14287	.1624	.18212	.2026	22.16

Table II.5: Mean and Variances of Borrowers' Discount Rate with $a=50$

$$a = 50, \quad \nu = 4, \quad \psi^2 = 100 r_m \ (= 2ar_m)$$

When the number of payments is finite, we could repeat our calculations for r_d. Analytical solutions are difficult, however. Using numerical techniques, reasonable estimates for the probability distribution of the rate of discount r_d as well as the probability moments can be obtained. For example, for T payments and $n = 1$

$$\bar{f}(r_d) = \frac{r_d e^{-ar_d}}{(1-e^{-r_d T}) \int_{r_m}^{\infty} \frac{r_d e^{-ar_d}}{(1-e^{-r_d T})} dr_d}$$

while the mean rate of discount is:

$$E\{r_d\} = \int_{r_m}^{\infty} \frac{T^2 r_d e^{-ar_d}}{(1-e^{-r_d T})} dr_d \bigg/ \int_{r_m}^{\infty} \frac{r_d e^{-ar_d}}{(1-e^{-r_d T})} dr_d$$

Such integrals are incomplete Zeta integrals and should be calculated numerically.

We turn our attention next to computing the expected consumers' and the borrowers' surplus at a given market rate r_m. This equals the residual value per dollar to all consumers (borrowers) at a given market rate r_m. It is the difference between the cost of credit and the credit cost consumers are willing to sustain in acquiring a product. For simplicity we consider first the infinite payment case. Both surpluses are then (dropping the subscripts in the integrals) given by;

$$S_c(r_m) = \int_{r_m}^{\infty} \frac{f(r)}{r} dr = \int_{r_m}^{\infty} \frac{na^{(1+1/n)} r^{n-1} e^{-ar^n}}{\Gamma(1+1/n)} dr_c$$

and

$$S_b(r_m) = \int_{r_m}^{\infty} \frac{\bar{f}(r)}{r} dr = E\{\frac{1}{r_d}\}$$

Again using the incomplete gamma function, we obtain explicit expressions for the expected consumer surplus. Namely,

$$S_c = \Gamma(\frac{1}{n}, ar_m^n) = Q(\psi^2|\nu) \Gamma(\frac{1}{n})$$

$$\psi^2 = 2ar_m^n \qquad \nu = \frac{2}{n}$$

For $n = 1$, we have for example $S_c = aQ(2ar_m|2)$ which is an incomplete gamma function of a -- the slope of the exponential demand curve -- and the market rate r_m. For the borrower's surplus, we find that

$$S_b = \frac{\Gamma(1/n,\ ar_m^n)}{\Gamma(1 + \frac{1}{n},\ ar_m^n)} = \frac{\Gamma(\frac{1}{n})}{\Gamma(1 + \frac{1}{n})} \cdot \frac{Q(\Psi^2/\nu_1)}{Q(\Psi^2/\nu_2)}$$

$$\Psi^2 = 2ar_m^n \qquad \nu_1 = 2/n \qquad \nu_2 = 2(1 + 1/n)$$

For $n = 1$, we obtain

$$S_b = \frac{a \cdot Q(\Psi^2/2)}{Q(\Psi^2/4)} = \frac{S_c}{Q(\Psi^2/4)}$$

which implies for $n = 1$ that $S_c/S_b = Q(\Psi^2|4)$. The ratio of consumer to borrower surplus is a chi-square integral with 4 degrees of freedom.

A numerical example for $a = 50$ computing the expected consumer and borrower surplus is enclosed in Table II.6. We note here that as r_m increases, the surplus decreases.

r_m	.10	.12	.14	.16	.18	.20
Ψ^2	10	12	14	16	18	20
$Q(\Psi^2/2)$	.00674	.00248	.00091	.00034	.00012	.00005
$Q(\Psi^2/4)$	.04043	.01735	.00730	.00302	.00123	.0005
S_c	.337	.124	.0455	.017	.006	.08025
S_b	8.335	7.147	6.233	5.63	4.878	0.5

Table II.6: Consumer's and Borrower's Surplus

$a = 50 \qquad \Psi^2 = 2ar_m$

(3) The Probability Distribution of a Consumer's Discount Rates In Acquiring a New Car

To demonstrate the results obtained in the previous section, we have considered a data sample of 1269 consumer credit transactions for new cars.[36] The transactions were sorted out as a function of both the market discount rate r_m and the number of payments. The results are given in Table II.7 and plotted as a semi-logarithmic scale in Figure II.12.

T \ r	9	10	11	12	13	14	15	16
36	52	181	477	224	71	81	7	10
30	7	8	11	5	3	0	1	0
18	6	14	40	11	10	3	0	0
12	4	7	16	7	2	2	0	1
Total	70	212	554	248	87	88	9	11

T	36	30	18	12
a(T)	77.3	64.96	64.74	82.67
N(T)	$e^{14.67}$	$e^{9.498}$	$e^{10.8}$	$e^{11.87}$
y	36r	30r	18r	12r
	2.14	2.12	3.58	6.88

Table II.7: The Number of Transaction

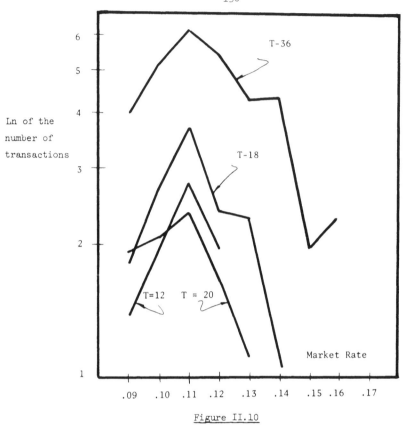

Figure II.10

The triangular shape of the curves in Figure II.10 correspond to the superposition[37] of the supply and the demand curves intersecting at $r = .11$. Considering only the demand side of the curve (the segment to the right of $r = .11$) we obtained the parameters $a(T)$ and $N(T)$ in Table II.7. Using these parameters we can obtain the probability distribution of consumer's discount rates. These probability distributions then express the "attitudes of consumers toward the future," reflected in the future payments they are willing to make for a consumption of goods now.

FOOTNOTES

1. In other words, decisions are made for short periods of time and are reviewed and changed often. In incremental planning the planning horizon involves the next or possibly a few subsequent periods.

2. Stability will be defined in greater detail in Chapter III. In the meantime we shall define a stabilizing decision strategy as one that can restore the state of the firm to equilibrium. A state of stability is reached, therefore, whenever we are and remain in equilibrium.

3. By assigning all of our resources to capacity expansion at a present time, we also run the risk of having a future demand not materialize. A partial commitment of these resources will obviously allow greater flexibility in meeting future opportunities.

4. We could also discuss planning problems in a conflicting environment, i.e., an environment involving opponents, raises several other problems which will not be discussed in this book. For further study see Von Neumann and Morgenstern (79), Telser (74), and Luce and Raiffa (36).

5. That is, planning as function of future expected states. If x is a random variable, with probability distribution $f(x)$, then $E(x) = \int x f(x) dx$ is the expected value on the basis of which we plan. Therefore, while x is a set of possible events, $E(x)$ is one presumed event which need not occur but which will most likely occur.

6. See Starr (59); White (81).

7. For a review of inventory theory and production control, see, for example, Naddor (38), Reisman and Buffa (47), Starr and Miller (60) and Wagner (80), Silver (54), Hadley and Whitin (26).

8. This is not to be confused with our more general understanding of memory. Here, memory will be defined in a very limited sense--a quantification of the states which can retrace the past.

9. That is, a differential delay process involves differential difference equations such as $dx(t)/dt = f(x(t), x(t-\tau))$. See Belman and Cooke (11).

10. See Tapiero and Farley (70).

11. See Toffler (77). Anticipative memory, however, does not relate to the future by an extrapolation of the past, but relates to the present by an "intrapolation" of the future. The distinction between "extrapolation" and "intrapolation" is extremely important as it indicates two radically different approaches to constructing the present.

12. See Shackle (53).

13. The solution is based on the mathematical appendix at the end of this chapter; see also Brown (13).

14. See Nerlove and Arrow (40), Nicosia (41), Schmalensee (51), Sasieni (50), and Tapiero (68) for example.

15. See Beer (10), Jastram (30) and Zielske (82).

16. For a review of the static transportation problem, see Wagner (80); also, for continuous time transportation models, see Tapiero (69), Tapiero and Soliman (71). For discrete analogs, see Frank (21) and Frank and El-Bardai (22).

17. A source i is not emptied at time T but at some time $T - \max_{j} \tau_{ij}$ where $\max_{j} \tau_{ij}$ is the maximum travel time from i to any destination j. Similarly, a destination is filled with a transported quantity at a time $T - \min_{i} \tau_{ij}$ where $\min_{i} \tau_{ij}$ is the minimum travel time from all sources i to the destination j.

18. The notation we used in this equation is defined as follows: $\forall\ i,j$: for all i and j; $\tau \in [-\tau_{ij}, 0]$ for time periods between τ_{ij} and zero.

19. Some noteworthy references are Bailey (5), Bartlett (7), Beckmann (8), Breiman (12). Cox and Miller (16), Cramer (17), Doob (18), Feller (20). Ito and McKean (29), Kuznetsov and Stratonovich (35), Mortensen (37), Pugachev (44), Saaty (49), Skorohod (55), Stratonovich (62), Tintner and Sengupta (76), Howard (28) and Kushner (34).

20. See a survey in Nelson (39), Einstein (19), Feller (20), and Ornstein and Uhlenbeck (42).

21. We shall not directly resolve partial differential equations in this book. For the solution of such equations, the reader is referred to an excellent survey by Sneddon (56).

22. When the distribution is discrete, we use the Kolmogorov equation which is a differential-difference equation to be discussed below. (See also Feller (20), Saaty (49), Bailey (5) and Bartlett (7) for further study.)

23. When the distribution is continuous, we use the Fokker-Planck equation which is a parabolic partial differential equation, also to be discussed below. (See Einstein (19), Nelson (39), Ornstein and Uhlenbeck (42).)

24. This will be discussed in far greater detail in Chapter V, section V.2.

25. That is, constructing a theoretical model and seeking some transaction probability parameters which indicate the best fit between the theoretical and empirical paths of a model. In Chapters III and IV, we shall return to these problems, called estimation and unknown parameters control problems.

26. For further study of stochastic differential equations the reader is referred to Doob (18), Ito and McKean (29), Kushner (34), Nelson (39), Skorohod (55), Stratonovich (62) as well as additional references on stochastic dynamic systems given in Chapter V.

27. This mean evolution is in fact the Vidale-Wolfe (78) model of advertising. See also Sethi (52) for an optimization study using this model. If we consider the dynamics of market share, we obtain Stigler's model (61).

28. The dynamic maintenance and replacement problem is an extremely old one. See, for example, Hotelling (27), Roos (48). More recent references are Tapiero (65), (66), (67).

29. An extensive and fundamental study of waiting lines is Saaty's outstanding book (49); see also Rau (45).

30. See, for example, Kessel (33).

31. The consumer surplus is defined here as the residual value of credit transactions when the market rate is r_m. The expected consumer surplus is then the integral over all consumers with discount rate probability greater than the market rate.

32. This is evident since $\partial D/\partial r = -\bar{D}nar^{n-1}e^{-ar^n}$ and $\int_0^\infty r\partial D/\partial r\,dr = -\bar{D}a\Gamma(1 + 1/n)/a^{(1+1/n)}$ with $\Gamma(1+1/n)$ defined as a gamma integral.

33. That is; $\int_0^\infty \dfrac{x^{q-1}e^{-\mu x}}{1-e^{-\beta x}}\,dx = \dfrac{\Gamma(q)}{\beta^q}\xi(q,\mu/\beta)$ where $\xi(q,\mu/\beta) = \sum_{n=0}^\infty \dfrac{1}{(n+\mu/\beta)^q}$. In our case, $q = 2$, $\mu = a$ and $\beta = T$.

34. This is evident since the pth moment is also a Riemann-Zeta integral with different parameters.

35. See Pearson and Hartley (43), Abramowitz and Stegun (1, p. 978).

36. These contracts were obtained by the Bureau of Consumer Protection of the Federal Trade Commission. Contracts included have represented auto dealerships selected by random procedures from among the 200 largest cities in the U.S.: (see Report of the Federal Trade Commission on Surveys of Creditor compliance with the Truth in Landing Act, April 1971 (mimeo.)

37. Both the theoretical justification and the empirical support for a triangular distribution of the quantities of credit related to its price and the rate of charge for credit, may be found in Consumer Credit in The United States, Report of the National Commission on Consumer Finance, December, 1972, pp. 109-113.

REFERENCES

1. Abramowitz, M. and I. A. Stegun, Handbook of Mathematical Functions, New York Dover Publications, 1965.

2. Allen, R.W., "Factors Influencing Market Penetration," Management Science, 13, 1966, 22-41.

3. Anasthassiades, J., "Sur les Solutions de L'equation Fontionnelle," $f(x+1) = \varphi(x)f(x)$," C.R. Acad. Sci., Nov. 20, 1961, pp. 2446-2447.

4. Arora, S.R. and P. T. Lele, "A Note on Optimal Maintenance Policy and Sale Date of a Machine," Management Science, 17, 1970, 170-174.

5. Bailey, N.T.J., The Elements of Stochastic Processes, New York, John Wiley & Sons Inc. 1964.

6. Barlow, R.E., F. Proschan and L.C. Hunter, Mathematical Theory of Reliability, New York, Wiley, 1965.

7. Bartlett, M.S., An Introduction to Stochastic Processes, Cambridge University Press, London, 1961.

8. Beckmann, P., Probability in Communication Engineering, New York, Harcourt, Brace & World Inc., 1967.

9. Beckman, M.J. and J.P. Wallace, "Continuous Lags and the Stability of Market Equilibrium," Economica, Feb. 1969, 58.

10. Beer, S., Cybernetics and Management Science, New York, Wiley, 1959.

11. Bellman, R. and K.L. Cooke, Differential-Difference Equations, New York, Academic Press, 1963.

12. Breiman, Leo, Probability and Stochastic Processes, New York, Houghton Mifflin Company, 1969.

13. Brown, R.G., Smoothing Forecasting and Prediction, Englewood Cliffs, N.J. Prentice Hall, 1963.

14. Capehart, B. L. and C. S. Bauer, "State Variable Methods for Digital Simulation of Economic and Inventory System Models," 38th National ORSA Meeting, Session GS3.15.

15. Champernowne, D.G., "Uncertainty and Estimation in Economics," Vol. I-III, Holden-Day, San Francisco, California, 1969.

16. Cox, D. R. and H. D. Miller, The Theory of Stochastic Processes, New York, Wiley 1965.

17. Cramer, H., "Model Building with the Aid of Stochastic Processes," *Technometrics*, 6, 1964, pp. 133-159.

18. Doob, J.L., *Stochastic Process*, New York, Wiley, 1953.

19. Einstein, A., *Investigations on the Theory of Brownian Movement*, New York, Dover Publications, 1956.

20. Feller, W., *An Introduction to Probability Theory and its Applications*, Vol. I & II, New York, Wiley, 1957, 1966.

21. Frank, H., "Dynamic Communication Networks," *IEEE Trans. on Communication Technology*, 1967, Conn-15, 156-163.

22. Frank H. and M.T. El-Bardai, "Dynamic Communications Networks with Capacity Constraints," *IEEE Trans. on Communication Technology*, Con. 17, 1969, 432-437.

23. Gillroy, J.G. & C.S. Tapiero, "Refining Capacity Expansion Planning in the Oil Industry," Mimeographed, Columbia University, 1973.

24. Gondolfo, Giancarlo, *Mathematical Methods and Models in Economic Dynamics*, North Holland Publishing Co., New York, American Elsvier Publishing Co., 1971.

25. Gradshteyn, I.S. and I.M. Ryzhik, *Table of Integrals, Series and Products*, New York, Academic Press, 1965.

26. Hadley, F. and T.H. Whitin, *Analysis of Inventory Systems*, Prentice Hall, Englewood Cliffs, N.J., 1963.

27. Hotelling, H., "A General Mathematical Theory of Depreciation," *The Journal of the Amer. Statistical Association*, 20, 1925, 340-353.

28. Howard, R.A., *Dynamic Programming and Markov Processes*, New York Wiley, 1960.

29. Ito, K. and H.P. McKean, "Diffusion Processes and Their Sample Paths," *N.Y. Academic Press*, 1967.

30. Jastram, R.W., "A Treatment of Distributed Lags in the Theory of Advertising," *Journal of Marketing*, 1955, 20, 36-46.

31. Johnson, N.L., and S. Kotz, *Discrete Distributions*, New York Houghton Mufflin Company, 1969.

32. Kamien, M.I. & N.I. Schwartz, "Optimal Maintenance and Sale Age for a Machine Subject to Failure," *Management Science*, 17, 1971, 495-504.

33. Kessel, R.A., "The Cyclical Behavior of the Term Structure of Interest Rates in J.M. Guttentag (ed.)", Essay on Interest Rates, New York, N.B.E.R., No. 93, 1971.

34. Kushner, H.J., "On the Differential Equations Satisfied by Conditional Probability Densities of Markov Processes, with Applications" J. SIAM Control, Ser. A, 2, 1964, 106-119.

35. Kuznetsov, P.I., R.L. Stratonovich, V.I. Tikhonov (Eds.), Non-Linear Transformation of Stochastic Processes, London, Pergamon Press, 1963.

36. Luce, R.D. and H. Raiffa, Games and Decisions, New York, Wiley, 1957.

37. Mortensen, R.E., "Mathematical Probelms of Modeling Stochastic Non-Linear Dynamic Systems," Journal of Statistical Physics, 1, 1969 271-296.

38. Naddor, E., Inventory Systems, New York, Wiley, 1966.

39. Nelson, E.A., Dynamical Theories of Brownian Motion, Princeton, N.J., Princeton University Press, 1967.

40. Nerlove, M. and K.J. Arrow, "Optimal Advertising Policy Under Dynamic Conditions," Economica, 39, 1962, 129-142.

41. Nicosia, F.M., Consumer Decision Processes: Marketing & Advertising Implications, Englewood Cliffs, N.J. Prentice Hall, 1966.

42. Ornstein, L.S. and G.E. Uhlenbeck, "On the Theory of the Brownian Motion," Physical Review, 36, 1930, 823-841.

43. Pearson, E.S. and H.O. Hartley (Eds.) Biometrika Tables for Statisticians, Vol. I, Cambridge, Cambridge University Press, England, 1954.

44. Pugachev, V.S., Theory of Random Functions and Its Application to Control Problems, London, Pergamon Press, 1965.

45. Rau, J.G., Optimization and Probability in Systems Engineering, New York, Van Nostrand Reinhold, Co. 1970.

46. Rashevsky, N., Mathematical Theory of Human Relations, Principia Press, Bloomington, (Indiana) 1948.

47. Reisman, A. and E.S. Buffa, "A General Model for Production and Operations Systems in E.S. Buffa (Ed.)" Readings in Production and Operations Management, New York, Wiley, 1966.

48. Roos, C.F., "A Mathematical Theory of Depreciation and Replacement," American J. of Mathematics, 50, 1928, 147-157.

49. Saaty, T.L., <u>Elements of Queueing Theory</u>, New York, McGraw Hill Book Co., 1961.

50. Sasieni, M.W., "Optimal Advertising Expenditure," <u>Management Science</u>, 18, 1971, 64-72.

51. Schmalensee, R., <u>The Economics of Advertising</u>, New York, North-Holland Publishing Co., 1972.

52. Sethi, S.P., "Optimal Control of the Vidale Wolfe Advertising Model," <u>Operations Research</u>, 21, 1973, 998-1013.

53. Shackle, G.L.S., <u>Time in Economics</u>, Amsterdam, North-Holland Publishing Co., 1958.

54. Silver, E.A., "A Tutorial on Production Smoothing and Work Force Balancing," <u>Operations Research</u>, 15, November-December, 1967.

55. Skorohod, A.V., <u>Studies in the Theory of Random Processes</u>, Addison-Wesley, N.Y., 1965.

56. Sneddon, I.N., <u>Elements of Partial Differential Equations</u>, New York, McGraw-Hill Book Co., 1957.

57. Soloviev, A.D., "Theory of Aging Elements," in L. Lecam, J. Neyman (eds.) <u>Proceedings of the Eighth Berkeley Symposium of Mathematical Statistics and Probability</u>, Vol. III Physical Sciences and Engineering, Berkeley, U. of California Press, 1967, pp. 313-324.

58. Starr, M.K., <u>Management: Modern Approach</u>; New York, Harcourt Brace & Jovanovitch, 1971.

59. Starr, M.K., A Quantitative Approach to Management Planning: Contingency Planning Models. Presented at the IESE Conference in Barcelona, Spain in June 1970 and published in Proceedings, 1971.

60. Starr, M.K. and D.W. Miller, <u>Inventory Control; Theory and Practice</u>, Englewood Cliffs, N.J. Prentice Hall, 1962.

61. Stigler, G.J., <u>The Organization of Industry</u>, R.D. Irwin, Inc. Homewood, Illinois, 1968.

62. Stratonovich, R.L., "A New Representation for Stochastic Integrals and Equations," <u>SIAM J. and Control</u>, 4, 1966, 362-371.

63. Tapiero, C.S., "Transportation-Location-Allocation, Over Time," <u>Journal of Regional Science</u>, 11, 1971, pp. 377-384.

64. Tapiero, C.S., "Transportation Over Time: A System Approach," Invited Paper Control Theory Session, XX International TIMS Meeting, June 1973, Tel-Aviv, Israel.

65. Tapiero, C.S., "Optimal Simultaneous Replacement and Maintenance of a Machine with Process Discontinuities," <u>R.I.R.O.</u>, 2, 1971, 79-86.

66. Tapiero, C.S., "Optimal Maintenance and Replacement of a Sequence of r-Machine and Technical Obselescence," Opsearch, 10, 1973, 1-13.

67. Tapiero, C.S., "Optimum Maintenance and Replacement Date of a Machine Under Uncertainty," Working Paper, Columbia University, 1974.

68. Tapiero, C.S., "Optimum Advertising and Goodwill Under Uncertainty," Working Paper No. 50, Columbia University, 1974.

69. Tapiero, C.S., "On-Line and Adaptive Optimum Advertising Control by a Diffusion Approximation, Operations Research, 22, 1975, 890-907.

70. Tapiero, C.S., "Random Walk Models of Advertising and Their Diffusion Approximation, and Hypothesis Testing", Annals of Economics and Social Measurement, 4, 1975, 293-309.

71. Tapiero, C.S. and I.U. Farley, "Optimal Control of Sales Effort Over Time," Management Science, 21, 1975, 976-985.

72. Tapiero, C.S. and M.A. Soliman, "Multi-Commodities Transportation Schedules Over Time," Network, 2, 1972, 311-327.

73. Tapiero, C.S. and R. Shay, "Buy Now-Pay Later, Credit Plans," Working Paper, Columbia University, 1974.

74. Teichroew, D., An Introduction to Management Science, New York, Wiley 1964.

75. Telser, L.G., Competition, Collusion and Game Theory, Chicago, Aldine Atherton, 1972.

76. Thompson, G.L., "Optimal Maintenance Policy and Sale Date of a Machine," Management Science, 14, 1968, 543-550.

77. Tintner, G. and S.K. Sengupta, Stochastic Economics; Stochastic Processes, Control and Programming, New York, Academic Press, 1972.

78. Toffler, A., Future Shock, New York, Bantam Bodes, 1971.

79. Vidale, M.L., and H.B. Wolfe, "An Operations Research Study of Sales Response to Advertising," Operations Research, 5, 1957, pp. 370-381.

80. Von Newman, J. and O. Morgenstern, Theory of Games and Economic Behavior, Princeton, Princeton University Press, New Jersey, 1944.

81. Wagner, H., "Principles of Operations Research," Englewood Cliffs, N.J. 1969.

82. White, D.J., "Problem Involving Infrequent but Significant Contingencies," Oper. Res. Quart., 20, 1969, 45-58.

83. Zielske, H.A., "The Remembering and Forgetting of Advertising," Journal of Marketing, Jan. 1959, 239-243.

Problems

1. Differentiate between plans, policies, strategies and tactics.

2. Categorize the following situations with respect to how stable their environment are likely to be and the degree of repetition that can be anticipated for the relevant environments: (i) plans for the expansion of accommodations for a ski lodge; (ii) the policies of the post office, concerning the amounts and types of mail that are delivered, and the price of postage stamps; (iii) planning changes in the size of the maternity ward in a large metropolitan hospital (Starr 58, p. 322).

3. How does timing relate to the following kinds of decision problems (i) the selection of a new site; (ii) the production of a new product design; (iii) the choice of a new President (Starr 58, p.240).

4. A monopolist advertises a product in a market which can absorb no more than M dollars of advertising per unit time. (i) Let $S(t)$ be the sales at time t, show that without advertising, sales evolve following the differential equation $dS/dt = mS$, $S(0) = S_0$, $m > 0$. What is the meaning of m? (ii) If the firm advertises, then $dS/dt = -mS+qa(M-S)$, $q > 0$, a equals the advertising rate in dollars, q is a parameter. Justify this equation and solve for S when the advertising rate is constant and when the advertising rate is given by a step function of step length T. (Teichroew 73).

5. A population of 1 million inhabitants increases to two millions in 50 years. How many years are required for the population to triple and quadruple if the growth rate of the population is proportional to the size of the population.

6. Growth curves are defined by the differential equation $dx/dt = f(x)$ where $f(x)$ is the growth rate. Find $x(t)$ and discuss the meaning of your solutions for (i) $f(x) = -a$, (ii) $f(x) = a-bx$, (iii) $f(x) = a+bx-x^2$ with $a > 0$ and $b > 0$.

7. Define the following variables: S = sales of a company in any year, C = sales of competition in any year, M = total market, M = available market ($= M-S-C$). Justify the following differential equations $dS/dt = a(M-S-C) - bS$, $dC/dt = c(M-S-C) - eC$ and explain the meaning of parameters a, b, c and e.

8. Let x be the size of a population of one type (e.g. supporting a candidate A for office), x_0 of which are firm supporters of that candidate. Let y be the size of a population for another type (e.g. not supporting candidate A), y_0 of which are firm opponents of this candidate. Let x, y be the number of persons susceptible to influence, $x = x-x_0$, $y = y-y_0$. Show that this can be modeled by a system of two differential equations $dx/dt = ax-by+c$, $dy/dt = ey-fx+g$ where a, b, c, e, f and g are positive numbers. (Rashevsky 46)

9. The equations describing the decision process of a consumer with respect to a brand x at time t are $dB/dt = b[M - \beta B]$, $M = mA$ $dA/dt = a[B - \alpha A] + cC$ where $B(t)$ = level of buying, $M(t)$ = motivation, $A(t)$ = consumer attitude, $C(t)$ = level of communication (e.g. advertising). a) Provide an analytical solution to $B(t)$ and $A(t)$, when $C(t)$ is a constant $\bar{C}$. b) Reformulate the relationships above in probabilistic terms and write down the equations for the equivalent stochastic process.

10. a) Consider the differential equation $dF/dt = c[F-A][B-F]$ where c, A and B are constants with $c > 0$, $B > A$. This can be interpreted as a rate of growth proportional to the excesses of two asymptotic values A and B. Show that a solution of this equation (a Ricatti differential equation) yields

$$F(t) = \frac{BDe^{t/c} + A}{De^{t/c} + 1}$$

where D is a constant. b) Compare this equation with the logistic distribution;

$$f_x(x) = (4\beta)^{-1} \text{sech}^2\{\tfrac{1}{2}(x-\alpha)/\beta\}$$

or in cumulative form;

$$F_x(x) = [1 + \exp\{-(x-\alpha)/\beta\}]^{-1}$$

$$= \tfrac{1}{2}[1 + \tanh\{\tfrac{1}{2}(x-\alpha)/\beta\}]$$

c) Suggest applications of this curve to describe growth phenomena.

11. Let the lifetime of an individual be defined by a probability distribution $p(T)$. The probability of surviving at least x is

$$\text{Prob}[T > x] = \int_x^\infty p(T)dT = 1 - F_T(x)$$

a) Compute the conditional probability that an individual having survived x will survive more than x+t. (answ. $[F_T(x+t) - F_T(x)]/t(1 - F_T(x))$). b) Show that as $t \to 0$, we obtain an "instantaneous death rate" at age x, given by:

$$p(x)[1 - F_T(x)]^{-1}$$

12. Define by D_t, S_t, P_t the demand, supply and price of a product at time t. Assume that the supply reacts with a delay of one period to price and that both demand and supply are linear functions of the price.

$$D_t = a + bp_t$$
$$S_t = \alpha + \beta p_{t-1}$$

Show that in conditions of equilibrium (supply equals demand), the evolution of prices is given by

$$p_t = (p_0 - p_e)(\beta/b)^t + p_e$$

where p_e equals $(\alpha-a)/(b-\beta)$ and p_0 is the initial price.

(ii) Supply decisions are based on an 'expected' price $\hat{p}_t$, where:
$$\hat{p}_t = p_{t-1} + \gamma(p_N - p_{t-1}) \qquad 0 < \gamma < 1$$
is a constant and p_N is some price used for forecasting purposes. Show that when $p_N = p_e$ that
$$p_t = (p_0 - p_e)(\beta(1-\gamma)/b)^t + p_e$$

(iii) Discuss the cases: a) $\beta(1-\gamma)/b < 1$; b) $\beta(1-\gamma)/b > 1$.
(iv) What is the effect of a constant γ upon the evolution of prices?
(v) If $a = 100$, $b = 2$, $\alpha = -20$, $\beta = 3$, compute the time path of prices as a function of the initial price p_0.
(vi) Now assume that expected prices evolve according to:
$$\hat{p}_t = p_{t-1} + \gamma(p_{t-1} - p_{t-2})$$
If $\gamma > 0$, the expectation is one of increasing prices
If $\gamma < 0$, the expectation is one of decreasing prices
Show that if supply decisions are based on expected price, then the equilibrium price is given by
$$p_e = (\alpha - a)/(b - \beta)$$
(vii) For what values of γ does the expected price converge towards the equilibrium price p_e.
(viii) Repeat computations with $a = 100$, $b = 2$, $\alpha = -20$, $\beta = 3$ and $\gamma = -1$, $-.5$, $0.$, $+.5$, 1. (Gondolfo 24).

13. a) In macro-economic theory, consumption C_t at time t is taken to be a linear function of the past income Y_{t-1}, $C_t = a + bY_{t-1}$. Using the identity $Y_t = C_t + S_t$ where S_t is the savings at time t, and assuming that savings equal investments I_t at time t, find the time path of income Y_t if $I_t = k(Y_t - Y_{t-1})$. b) If savings S_t are given by sY_t, show that $Y_t = Y_0(1 + s/k)^t$. c) Repeat a, b, by letting $a = 50$, $b = .60$. d) Repeat the problem in a by assuming that the consumption function is given as a function of the last 3 periods.
$$C_t = a + \sum_{j=1}^{3} b^j Y_{t-j} \qquad 0 < b < 1$$
where $a = 50$, $b = .60$.

14. Assume that the demand for a product at time t is given by $D(t)$ and let $P(t)$ be its price. Define a linear demand function $D(t) = \alpha + aP(t)$ and let the supply $S(t)$ depend on "expected" prices. These expected prices are given by distributed lags
$$S(t) = \beta + b \int_{-\infty}^{t} w(t-\tau) P(\tau) d\tau$$
When the market is in equilibrium; $D(t) = S(t)$, show that;
$$P(t) = \frac{\beta - \alpha}{a} + \frac{b}{a} \int_{-\infty}^{t} w(t-\tau) P(\tau) d\tau$$

Show that an equilibrium solution exists if $\int^{\infty} w(\tau)d\tau$ is finite and demonstrate that if $\bar{P}$ is the equilibrium price and $p(t) = P(t) - \bar{P}$, then

$$p(t) = f(t) + \int_0^t a(t-\tau)p(\tau)d\tau$$

with $a(\tau) = (b/a)w(\tau)$ and $f(t)$ is a known function of current prices. (Beckmann and Wallace 9).

15. Pearson's equation in probability theory is given by:

$$\frac{dy}{dx} = (\delta-x)y/(\alpha + \beta x + \gamma x^2)$$

a. What type of differential equation is this?
b. Make the following assumptions,
   (i) $\beta = \gamma = $ $\alpha > 0$
   (ii) $\alpha = \gamma = \delta = 0$ $\beta > 0$
   (iii) $\alpha = \gamma = 0$ $\beta > 0$ $\delta > -\beta$
   (iv) $\alpha = 0$, $\beta = -\gamma$ $\delta > 1-\beta$

and integrate the resultant probability distribution. What is the name of each of the resultant probability distributions you have found?

16. Consider the difference equation

$$\Delta f_{r-1} = (a-r)f_{r-1}/(b_0 + b_1 r + b_2 r(r-1))$$

A solution to this equation contains various hypergeometric distributions, the two binomials, the Poisson and the discrete student t-distribution. Obtain as many solutions to this equation as you can by making your own assumptions concerning the parameters a, b_0, b_1 and b_2.

17. Let $f(x+1) = (x/(x+y))f(x)$ $y > 0$ and $f(1) = 1/y$ and $f(x)$ is a decreasing function. Show that

                 $f(x) = \Gamma(x)\Gamma(y)/\Gamma(x+y)$
or $f(x) = B(x,y) = B(y,x)$ where $B(x,y)$ is the Beta function

18. Assume that a machine at age t has a probability $\lambda(t)\Delta t$ of failing in a small time interval of length t. Say that $R(t)$ is the probability that the machine reaches an age t. Show that for infinitesimal intervals show that $R(t)$ is given by

$$R(t) = \exp[\int_0^t \lambda(\tau)d\tau]$$

with $R(0) = 1$. This result is one of the fundamental results in reliability theory.

19. Consider the following model

$$S(t) = y(t)$$
$$I(t) = dy/dt \quad y(0) = y^0$$
$$S(t) = I(t)$$
$$\alpha > 0, \quad \beta > 0$$

where S = savings, I = investment, y = income

(a) Explain the meaning of each of these equations
(b) Explain the meaning of the model in economic terms and in mathematical terms
(c) Show that the solution for y, I and S yields

$$y = y^0 \exp(\alpha/\beta)t$$
$$I = S = \alpha y^0 \exp(\alpha/\beta)t$$

20. Assume that T, the planning horizon of a person is given by;

(i) T = W+V where W and V are given constants
(ii) T is a rectangular variate

$$W < T < W+2V$$

i.e., T has uniform probability distribution $\frac{1}{2}V$ with mean W+V.

Say that $u(x_t)$ is the value derived from a product at time t. Show how we can compute the value of the product over its life time in both case (i) and (ii). (Champernowne 15)

21. Define the reliability of a system of time t as the proportion of elements in that system which has not failed. That is, if

$N_0(t)$: number of operating elements at time t
$N_F(t)$: number of failed elements at time t
$N(t)$: total number of elements $(N = N_0(t) + N_F(t))$
$R(t)$: reliability at time t.

$$R(t) = \frac{N_0(t)}{N} = 1 - \frac{N_F(t)}{N}$$

Deriving both sides of the equation with respect to time:

$$\frac{dR(t)}{dt} = -\frac{1}{N}\frac{dN_F(t)}{dt}$$

and

$$r(t) = \frac{1}{N_0(t)}\frac{dN_F(t)}{dt} = \frac{-N}{N_0(t)}\frac{dR(t)}{dt} = \frac{-dR(t)}{R(t)dt}$$

where r(t) is the rate of function failure,

a. Show that $R(t) = \exp(-\int_0^t r(\tau)d\tau)$

b. If the system has a failure time distribution with probability density f(t), then the failure time distribution function is given by

$$F(t) = \int_0^t f(\tau)d\tau$$

which is called the unreliability of the system at time t.

Reliability is thus
$$R(t) = 1 - F(t) = \exp\left(-\int_0^t r(\tau)d\tau\right)$$
Show that
$$r(t) = f(t)/[1 - F(t)]$$

c. Compute the reliability functions of the system when:
1) $f(t) = \lambda e^{-\lambda t}$ (answer $r(t) = \lambda$, $R(t) = e^{-\lambda t}$)
2) $f(t) = \lambda \alpha t^{\alpha-1} e^{-\lambda t^\alpha}$ (answer $r(t) = \lambda \alpha t^{\alpha-1}$, $R(t) = e^{-\lambda t^\alpha}$) $\alpha, \lambda > 0$
3) $f(t) = \dfrac{\lambda}{(r-1)!} (\lambda t)^{r-1} e^{-\lambda t}$

r positive integer

(Answer $r(t) = \dfrac{\lambda^r t^{r-1}}{(r-1)!} \dfrac{e^{-\lambda t}}{R(t)}$, $R(t) = \sum\limits_{j=0}^{r-1} \dfrac{(\lambda t)^j e^{-\lambda t}}{j!}$ (Rau 45)

22. Solve for x and y if:
$$\frac{dx}{dt} = 2x - y - 5 \qquad \frac{dy}{dt} = 3y - 2x + 4$$

23. Indicate the type and solve the following differential equations:

a. $\dfrac{dx}{dt} = (\alpha - x)(\beta - x)$

b. $\dfrac{dx}{dt} - 2 + t = 0$

c. $\dfrac{dx}{dt} + 2xt = 1 + 2t^2$

d. $\dfrac{dx}{dt} + 2x = 2t^2 - 3t + 5$

e. $t\dfrac{dx}{dt} - x = \dfrac{-x^3}{4}$

24. Let P(t) be the price of a product at time t. The demand D(t), given as a function of time and price is given by an ordinary differential equation;
$$D(t) = F(t, P, dP/dt)$$
Discuss possible forms for F and indicate from logical reasoning what the signs of the parameters may be in your differential equation.

25. Clairaut's differential equation is of the following form:
$$x = t\frac{dx}{dt} + F\left(\frac{dx}{dt}\right)$$
Find the solution of this differential equation by first deriving this equation with respect to t and showing that
$$\frac{dy}{dt}\left[t + \frac{dF}{dt}(y)\right] = 0$$
where $y = dx/dt$.

26. Consider x_n as the number of occurrences of a particular event in the time interval $(0, n\Delta t]$ and assume that
$$P(x_n = k) = \binom{n}{k} p^k q^{n-k} \quad k = 0, 1, 2, \ldots, n$$
Show that z_n, the random variable denoting the time interval between the $(n-1)$th and n the event is given by
$$P(z_n = k) = q^{k-1} p \quad k = 1, 2, 3, \ldots$$
which is a geometric probability distribution with parameter p. Show also that the probability distribution until the n occurrence is negative binomial
$$P(Y_n = k) = \binom{k-1}{n-1} p^n q^{k-n}$$
$$E(Y_n) = n/p \quad \text{var}(Y_n) = nq/p^2$$

27. If x_n is a Poisson probability distribution
$$P_n(t) = e^{-\lambda t} (\lambda t)^n / n!$$
where λ is an arrival rate of passengers into a station. Show that the probability distribution of interarrival time is the negative exponential
$$p[z_n \leq \tau] = 1 - e^{-\lambda \tau} \quad \text{and}$$
$$p(z_n) = \lambda e^{-\lambda x}$$
Using these results show that the probability distribution of the time required to n events to occur is gamma
$$f(y) = \frac{e^{-\lambda y} \lambda^n y^{n-1}}{(n-1)!}$$

28. In example II.12, show that if the transition probabilities are $\lambda_n = \lambda$ and $\mu_n = n^c \mu$ then the long-run probability distribution of n is;
$$P_0 = \left[\sum_{n=0}^{\infty} \rho^n / (n!)^c \right]^{-1}$$
and
$$P_n = [\rho^n / (n!)^c] \pi_0 \quad \text{where} \quad \rho = \lambda / \mu$$
If $c = 1$, show that this is reduced to
$$P_n = e^{-\rho} \rho^n / n!$$

29. The M/M/s queueing system is given by the following transition probabilities

$$\mu_n = \begin{cases} s\mu & n > s \\ n\mu & n \leq s \end{cases}$$

a) Show that as $t \to \infty$ that

$$P_n = \frac{s^s \rho^n}{s!} P_0$$

$$P_0^{-1} = \sum_{r=0}^{s} \frac{(s\rho)^r}{r!} + \frac{\rho^{s+1} s^s}{s!} (1-\rho)^{-1}$$

and

$$\rho = \lambda/s\mu < 1$$

b) Show also that the expected queue length is given by;

$$E(Q) = s\rho + \frac{\rho \pi_s}{1-\rho^2}$$

c) Compare and obtain as specific cases, the M/M/1, M/M/2 and M/M/3 queueing systems.

30. Consider the transition probability

$$\lambda_n = \lambda/n+1; \quad \mu_n = \mu$$

Show that the long-run probability of the number of persons in a system is Poisson with

$$P_n = \frac{e^{-\rho} \rho^n}{n!} \quad \rho = \frac{\lambda}{\mu}$$

$$n = 0, 1, 2,\ldots$$

31. If $\lambda_n = \lambda$; $\mu_n = n$ $n \geq 0$, show that in the long run

$$P_n = \frac{e^{-\rho} \rho^n}{n!} \quad \rho = \lambda/\mu$$

32. Machine Minding with s repairmen. Show that if

$$\lambda_n = (M-n)\lambda \qquad n \leq M$$

$$\mu_n = \begin{cases} n\mu & \text{if } 1 \leq n < s \\ s\mu & \text{if } n \geq s \end{cases}$$

a) Then the long-run probabilities are

$$P_n = \binom{M}{n} \frac{n!}{s! s^{n-s}} \rho^n P_0 \qquad s \leq n \leq M$$

$$P_n = \binom{M}{n} \rho^n P_0 \qquad 0 \leq n \leq s$$

$$\rho = \lambda/\mu$$

where P_0 is found by the condition that $\sum_{n=0}^{M} P_n = 1$.

b) When $s = 1$, show that

$$P_n = \frac{M!}{(M-n)!} \rho^n P_0$$

33. The Ehrenfest random walk model of diffusion is given by:

$$P_{i,i-1} = \frac{1}{2}(1 + \frac{i}{a}) \qquad P_{i,i+1} = \frac{1}{2}(1 - \frac{i}{a})$$

$$P_{a,a-1} = 1, \quad P_{-a,-a+1} = 1 \qquad -a < i < a$$

Show that this can be described by a Fokker-Planck diffusion equation;

$$\frac{\partial f}{\partial t} = \beta \frac{\partial}{\partial x}(xf) + D \frac{\partial^2 f}{\partial x^2}$$

where $\beta = 1/a$ and $D = (1 + 1/a)$ and appropriate restrictions at the boundary. If $a \to \infty$, show that we obtain the simple Wiener process with $D = 1$;

$$\frac{\partial f}{\partial t} = \frac{\partial^2 f}{\partial x^2}$$

34. Consider the diffusion equation

$$\frac{\partial f}{\partial t} = -\frac{\alpha \partial}{\partial x}(xf) + \beta \frac{\partial^2}{\partial x^2}(xf)$$

with $f(x_0, 0, t) = 0$. Verify the solution

$$f(x_0, x, t) = \gamma \left(\frac{m}{x}\right)^{1/2} e^{-\gamma(x+m)} I_1(2\gamma\sqrt{xm}) \qquad 0 < x < \infty$$

where $I_1(x)$ is the Bessel function

$$I_1(x) = \sum_{n=0}^{\infty} \frac{(x/2)^{2n+1}}{n!(n+1)!}$$

$m = x_0 e^{\alpha t}$ and $\gamma = \alpha/\beta(e^{\alpha t} - 1)$. Show also that the mean and variance are given by m and $2e^{\alpha t}/\gamma$ respectively. (Feller 20)

35. A one absorbing barrier random walk model is given by
$$P_{i,i+1} = p \quad P_{i,i-1} = q \quad P_{00} = j \quad i = 1, 2,\ldots$$
    (a) Find a discrete time model of the diffusion process
    (b) Find the continuous time model
    $$\partial f/\partial t = \partial/\partial x(af) + 1/2 \partial^2/\partial x^2 (bf)$$
    (c) Verify the solution
    $$g(x,t) = (2\pi bt)^{-1/2} \{e^{-x^2/2b} - e^{-(x-2d)^2/2bt}\} \cdot \{e^{ax-a^2t/2b}\}$$

36. A two-absorbing barrier model is given by
$$P_{i,i+1} = p \quad P_{i,i-1} = q \quad P_{00} = 1 \quad P_{NN} = 1 \quad i = 1, 2,\ldots,N-1$$
    Show that the Fokker-Plank partial differential equation is of the form
    $$\frac{\partial f}{\partial t} = \frac{\partial}{\partial x}(af) + \frac{1}{2}\frac{\partial^2}{\partial x^2}(bf)$$
    Show that the solution
    $$g(x,t) = \sum_{j=-\infty}^{\infty} (-1)^j (2\pi bt)^{-1/2} \exp\{\frac{x-2d)^2}{2bt}\} \exp\{ax - \frac{a^2 t}{2b}\}$$
    verifies such a partial differential equation.

37. Show that a one-reflecting barrier and a two-reflecting barrier model can be defined by
    $$P_{i,i+1} = p \quad P_{i,i-1} = q \quad P_{00} = q \quad P_{01} = p \quad i = 1, 2,\ldots$$
    and
    $$P_{i,i+1} = p \quad P_{i,i-1} = q \quad P_{00} = q \quad P_{01} = p$$
    $$P_{NN} = p \quad P_{N,N-1} = q \quad i = 1, 2,\ldots,N-1$$

38. Describe the differences between the following prediction mechanisms
    a. $\hat{y}_t = a_t + \varepsilon_t$
    b. $\hat{y}_t = a_t y_{t-1} + \varepsilon_t$
    c. $\hat{y}_t = a(x_t) + \varepsilon_t$
       where x_t is a variable predicted by some other mechanisms.

39. Evans' model of price-quantity is given by
$$x(t) = b + ap(t) + hdp(t)/dt$$
where
$x(t)$ = quantity at time t
$p(t)$ = price at time t

Construct a similar model as a stochastic process where the probability of price change is given by transition probabilties which may be function of $x(t)$.

40. Show that the function
$$d(t) = \sum_{j=1}^{m} \alpha_j \rho_j^t \, t^{n_j} \exp[it\beta_j]$$
where α_j, ρ_j are real, n_j is an integer and β_j a complex number (i.e. $i = \sqrt{-1}$) can be written as $dw/dt = Aw(t)$, $d(t) = Kw(t)$ A, K constants.

Appendix II.1: Differential Equations

An equation relating two variables by a function of their derivatives is called an <u>ordinary differential equation</u> (abbreviated o.d.e.). The degree of an o.d.e. is given by the highest derivative it contains. For example,

$$F(t, x, dx/dt) = 0$$

is a first-order o.d.e.; and

$$F(t, x, dx/dt, d^2x/dt^2, \ldots, d^nx/dt^n) = 0$$

is an nth-order o.d.e. There are different types and forms of differential equations. For example, an o.d.e. can be separable, homogeneous, linear, or nonlinear. These equations are defined in Table A.1 below.

Differential Equation	Definition	Example
Separable	O.d.e. which can be reduced to $F_1(x)dx = F_2(t)dt$	$4x^2 dx/dt = (t^2-5)^2$
Homogeneous	O.d.e. which can be reduced to $dx/dt = F(x/t)$	$x^2 dx + (x^2-xt)dt = 0$
Linear	O.d.e. which is of the form $dx/dt + xF_1(t) = F_2(t)$	$dx/dt = 4tx + e^{6t}$
Nonlinear	O.d.e. which is of the form $dx/dt + F_1(t,x,dx/dt) = F_2(t,x,dx/dt)$	$dx/dt + 6t = (dx/dt)^2$

<u>Table A.1</u>: First Order Ordinary Differential Equations

A solution to an o.d.e. consists in finding a function which satisfies the differential equation. Because analytical solutions are difficult to find, except for some simple linear differential equations, we use numerical methods which allow differential equations to be solved on computers. In this appendix some elements in the solution of ordinary differential equations will be briefly reviewed. In particular, attention will be given to the solution of linear o.d.e.'s, to special forms of nonlinear o.d.e.'s, and to systems of simultaneous linear differential equations. For simplicity, we drop the time subscripts in the o.d.e.'s.

(1) Solution of Separable O.D.E.'s: A separable o.d.e. can be reduced to the form $F_1(x)dx = F_2(t)dt$. A solution, therefore, is obtained by integrating both sides of the equation so that $\int F_1(x)dx = \int F_2(t)dt$.

(2) Solution of Homogeneous Equations: These are o.d.e. which can be reduced to the form $dx/dt = F(x/t)$. This suggests the following change in variables: $v = x/t$. Deriving v with respect to t yields: $dx/dt = t\ dv/dt + v$. Inserting into the original equation, we obtain a separable differential equation. That is, $dv/[F(v) - v] = dt/t$ and $\int dv/[F(v) - v] = \log t$. Given a solution for v, x is found by $x = vt$.

(3) Solution of Linear Differential Equations: There are many types of linear differential equations; each type is distinguished by the order and degree of the differential equation. The order was defined earlier as the highest derivative in the o.d.e.; the _degree_ is defined as the highest power of the variable to be integrated. We shall now determine

a solution for linear o.d.e.'s of the first and n-th order as well as a solution to special differential equations named after Bernoulli and Ricatti.

(a) Solution of $dx/dt + F_1(t)x = F_2(t)$

To resolve this equation we introduce a change of variables $x = uv$ where u and v are two unknown functions of t. A derivative with respect to t yields $dx/dt = udv/dt + du/dtv$ and $udv/dt + du/dtv + F_1(t)uv = F_2(t)$. Rearranging the terms of this equation,

$$v[du/dt + F_1(t)u] + u\, dv/dt = F_2(t)$$

A u satisfying the differential equation in the brackets can be found by letting

$$du/dt + F_1(t)u = 0$$

This is a separable linear o.d.e. whose simplest solution is

$$e^{-\int F_1(t)dt} dv/dt = F_2(t)$$

which is again a separable linear o.d.e. The solution for v is therefore

$$v = \int e^{-\int F_1(t)dt} F_2(t)dt + C$$

Since $x = uv$, a solution for x is:

$$x(t) = \{e^{-\int F_1(t)dt}\}\{\int e^{+\int F_1(t)dt} F_2(t)dt + C\}$$

where C is an arbitrary constant.

(b) Solution of Bernoulli's Equation:

$$dx/dt + F_1(t)x = F_2(t)x^n, \qquad n \neq 0,1$$

A solution to this o.d.e. of the first order and the nth degree is found by a change in variables: $y = x^{1-n}$. Then, $dy/dt = (1-n)x^{-n}dx/dt$. Substituting in Bernoulli's equation, we obtain

$$dy/dt - (n-1)F_1(t)y = -(n-1)F_2(t)$$

which is an o.d.e. of the first order and first degree resolved earlier.

(c) **Solution of Ricatti's differential equation**

$$dx/dt = A(t)x^2 + B(t)x + C(t)$$

The Ricatti differential equation appears frequently in the calculus of variations and in optimum-control theory, as will be seen in Chapters IV and V. Although a general solution is difficult, special cases are worth pointing out.

<u>Case 1</u>: $A(t) = 0$: We obtain the linear o.d.e. of the first order and first degree.

<u>Case 2</u>: $C(t) = 0$: We obtain the Bernoulli o.d.e.

<u>Case 3</u>. $A(t) = A$, $B(t) = B$, $C(t) = C$ with A,B,C, constants: We obtain a solution by simple integration. That is,

$$\int dx/Ax^2 + bx + C = \int dt$$

<u>Case 4</u>: General case: To obtain a solution it is first necessary to "guess" a function which satisfies the Ricatti o.d.e. Let y_1 be this function; that is,

$$dy_1/dt = A(t)y_1^2 + B(t)y_1 + C(t)$$

Let $x = y_1 + y_2$ be the general solution. Then,

$$dx/dt = dy_1/dt + dy_2/dt = A(t)(y_1 + y_2)^2 + B(t)(y_1 + y_2) + C(t)$$

or

$$dy_1/dt + dy_2/dt = A(t)y_1^2 + B(t)y_1 + C(t) + A(t)y_2^2 + [2A(t)y_1 + B(t)]y_2$$

Since dy_1/dt is already a solution, we obtain

$$dy_2/dt = A(t)y_2^2 + [2A(t)y_1 + B(t)]y_2$$

This last equation is a Bernoulli o.d.e. whose solution was indicated earlier. Given y_2, a solution for x is then given by $x = y_1 + y_2$.

(d) Systems of simultaneous linear differential equations

Systems of simultaneous linear differential equations are defined by:

$$\frac{dx_1}{dt} = a_{11}x_1(t) + a_{12}x_2(t) + \ldots a_{1n}x_n(t) + b_{11}u_1(t) + \ldots b_{1m}u_m(t)$$

$$\vdots$$

$$\frac{dx_n}{dt} = a_{n1}x_1(t) + a_{n2}x_2(t) + \ldots a_{nn}x_n(t) + b_{n1}u_1(t) + \ldots b_{nm}u_m(t)$$

If $X(t) = [x_1(t), x_2(t), \ldots, x_n(t)]$ and $U(t) = [u_1(t), \ldots, u_m(t)]$

$$A = \begin{vmatrix} a_{11} & \cdots & a_{1n} \\ \vdots & & \\ a_{n1} & \cdots & a_{nn} \end{vmatrix} \qquad B = \begin{vmatrix} b_{11} & \cdots & b_{1m} \\ \vdots & & \\ b_{n1} & \cdots & b_{nm} \end{vmatrix}$$

Then in vector and matrix notation, the system of simultaneous linear differential equations can be written as:

$$\frac{dX(t)}{dt} = AX(t) + BU(t)$$

where

$X(t)$ = state vector ($n \times 1$)

A = the system matrix ($n \times n$)

B = input distribution matrix ($n \times m$)

$U(t)$ = input vector ($m \times 1$)

The solution to this equation when A, B are constants is given by:

$$X(t) = \Phi(t, t_0)X(t_0) + \int_{t_0}^{t} \Phi(t,\tau)BU(\tau)d\tau$$

where $\Phi(t, t_0)$ is called the <u>state transition matrix</u>. When A is constant

$$\Phi(t, t_0) = e^{A(t-t_0)}$$

where $e^{A(t-t_0)} = \sum_{y=0}^{\infty} A^j \frac{(t-t_0)^j}{j!}$ which is the Taylor series expansion for

$\Phi(t,t_0)$. The computation of $\exp[A(t-t_0)]$. is a fairly simple task when A, B are constants. When $A(t)$, $B(t)$ are time-variable, we rewrite the differential equation as

$$\frac{dX'(t)}{dt} = F(t)X'(t)$$

If we let $F(t) = F(kT) = F_k$ for $kT \leq t \leq kT + T$ then, for each sample period,

$$X'(t) = e^{F_0(t-t_0)} X'(0) \qquad t_0 \leq t < T$$

$$X'(2t) = e^{F_1(t-T)} X'(T) \qquad T \leq t < 2T$$

$$X'(k+1) = e^{F_k(t-kT)} X'(T) \qquad kT \leq t < kT+T$$

and at each sampling time it is necessary to compute F_k, $k = 0, 1, 2,...$ by

$$\sum_{j=0}^{\infty} \frac{F_{k+1}^j (t-kT)^j}{j!}$$

To compute this function we can use a matrix exponential subroutine (see Capehart and Bauer [14] for example).

Appendix II.2: Stochastic Calculus

This appendix provides elementary notions of stochastic calculus. The reader is referred to [7, 18, 29, 34, 62] at the end of this chapter as well as to references on filtering and stochastic control in Chapter V (in particular see Jazwinsky's book). We shall seek below a definition of stochastic integrals and differential equations and provide the essential theorems of an Ito stochastic calculus.

We consider continuous time, continuous state stochastic processes $\{x(t); t \geq 0\}$ with finite second moment. Define the correlation function $B(t,\tau)$ describing the correlation between $x(t)$ and $x(\tau)$. A random function $x(t)$ is said to be continuous in a mean square sense at $t \in T$, if and only if $B(t,\tau)$ is continuous at every (t,τ) point. The implications of this continuity are that: (l.i.m $\equiv$ limit in mean) $\text{l.i.m}_{\Delta t \to 0} x(t+\Delta t) = x(t)$ which implies $\text{l.i.m.} |x(t+\Delta t) - x(t)|^2 \to 0$ as $\Delta t \to 0$. Further for t, $\tau \in T$, we note that $\text{l.i.m.} |x(t+\Delta t) - x(\tau+\Delta\tau)|^2 = E(x(t)x(\tau))$ as $\Delta t \to 0$, $\Delta \tau \to 0$ (see Doob [18] for proofs).

The random function $x(t)$ is called mean-square differentiable at $t \in T$ if the following limit exists;

$$\lim_{\Delta t \to 0} \frac{x(t+\Delta t) - x(t)}{\Delta t} \equiv \frac{dx(t)}{dt}$$

Evidently, a mean-square differentiable function is also mean-square continuous since

$$\lim_{\Delta t \to 0} x(t+\Delta t) - x(t) = \frac{[(dx(t)]}{(dt)} dt + O(R)$$

where $O(R)$ is a remainder which tends to zero faster than dt (as dt tends to zero). Thus,

$$\lim_{\Delta t \to 0} |x(t+\Delta t) - x(t)|^2 = E[\frac{dx(t)^2}{(dt)} (dt)^2] = O(R)$$

which is the definition used above for mean-square continuous functions. We can use similar procedures to define a m.s.R. (mean-square Riemann) integrable random function on $T = [t_0, T]$. Specifically,

(1) partition the interval $T-t_0$ in N steps of lengths $t_{j+1} - t_j$ with $\rho = \max_j (t_{j+1} - t_j)$ $j = 1, \ldots, N-1$, $t_N = T$ and

(2) define the limit for all partitions of T
$$\lim_{\rho \to 0} \sum_{j=0}^{N-1} x(t_j)[t_{j+1} - t_j] = \int_{t_0}^{T} x(t) dt$$

If this limit exists, the random function $x(t)$ is said to be m.s.R. integrable. Such a function also has a Riemann integrable and continuous correlation $B(t,\tau)$. From these definitions it follows that if

$$y(t) = \int_{t_0}^{t} x(\tau) d\tau$$

and if $x(t)$ is m.s.R. integrable, then $y(t)$ is m.s.R. differentiable and

$$\frac{dy(t)}{dt} = x(t)$$

From the foregoing we obtain the fundamental theorem of mean-square calculus.

<u>Theorem</u>

If $dx(t)/dt$ is m.s.R. integrable, then

$$x(t) - x(t_0) = \int_{t_0}^{t} \frac{(dx(t))}{(dt)} dt \text{ with probability 1}$$

Proofs for this theorem and subsequent ones can be found in the book of Jazwinsky, we refer to in Chapter V.

Now consider the stochastic differential equation (with time subscript dropped for x and t),

$$dx/dt = f(x,t) + g(x,t)\xi(t)$$

Using the fundamental theorem of mean square calculus,

$$x(t) - x(t_0) = \int_{t_0}^{t} \frac{(dx)}{(dt)} dt = \int_{t_0}^{t} f(x,t) dt + \int_{t_0}^{t} g(x,t) \xi dt$$

If the function f is mean-square continuous, then the first integral $\int f dt$ is m.s.R. integrable. When ξ is a white gaussian process, and therefore unbounded, the second integral $\int g \xi dt$ is not m.s.R. integrable. We define

$$\xi(t) \sim \frac{d\beta(t)}{dt} \quad \text{and} \quad \xi(t) dt = d\beta(t)$$

where $\beta(t)$ is a Wiener-Levy process (or Brownian motion). Rewrite the last integral equation;

$$x(t) - x(t_0) = \int_{t_0}^{t} f(x,t) dt + \int g(x,t) d\beta(t)$$

and call $\int g d\beta$ a stochastic integral. On page 106, we provided two definitions for such integrals -- Ito's and Stratonovich's. We shall use Ito's definition and denote stochastic integrals by f.

Define the partition $t_{j+1} - t_j$, $t_N = T$, and the corresponding step functions;

$$g(x,t) = \begin{cases} 0 & \text{if } t < t_0 \\ g(x, t_j) & \text{if } t_j < t < t_{j+1} \\ 0 & \text{if } t \geq t_N \end{cases}$$

For such step functions, the stochastic integral is then given by:

$$f_T g(x,t) d\beta(t) = \sum_{j=0}^{N-1} g(x,t_j) [\beta(t_{j+1}) - \beta(t_j)]$$

Below we summarize the essential theorems which relate to the existence of Ito's stochastic integrals, solutions of stochastic differential equations, and theorems of stochastic calculus.

Theorem: Itô's Stochastic Integral

Let $\rho = \max_j(t_{j+1} - t_j)$ on a partition of T,

T: $t_0 < t_1 < t_2 \ldots < t_{j+1} < \ldots t_N = T$.

Let $g(x,t)$, a random function, be mean-square continuous on T and be statistically independent of $[\beta(t_{j+1}) - \beta(t_j)]$, where $\beta(t)$ is a Wiener-Levy process with variance $\sigma^2(x,t)$. Finally, let $E(g(x,t)^2)$ be finite for all $t \in T$. Then the Itô stochastic integral equals the mean-square limit.

$$\underset{\rho \to 0}{\text{l.i.m.}} \sum_{j=0}^{N-1} g(x, t_j)[\beta(t_{j+1}) - \beta(t_j)] = \int_T g(x,t) d\beta(t)$$

Theorem: Existence of Solution of Stochastic Differential Equations.

Suppose that a stochastic differential is given by;

$$dx = f(x,t)dt + g(x,t)d\beta \quad \text{on} \quad t_0 \leq t \leq T$$

where the real functions f and g and the initial condition $x(t_0)$ satisfy the hypotheses given below:

(1) f and g satisfy uniform Lipschitz conditions in x. That is, there is a $K > 0$ such that for x_2 and x_1,

$$|f(x_2,t) - f(x_1,t)| \leq K|x_2 - x_1|$$
$$|g(x_2,t) - g(x_1,t)| \leq K|x_2 - x_1|$$

(2) f and g are continuous in t on $[t_0, T]$

(3) $x(t_0)$ is any random variable with $E|x(t_0)|^2 < \infty$, independent of the increment stochastic process $\{d\beta(t), t \in [t_0, T]\}$.

Then,

(1) The stochastic differential equation has, in the mean square sense, a solution on $t \in [t_0, T]$, given by

$$x(t) - x(t_0) = \int_{t_0}^{t} f(x,\tau)d\tau + \int_{t_0}^{t} g(x,\tau)d\beta(\tau)$$

(2) $x(t)$ is mean square continuous on $[t_0, T]$

(3) $E[|x(t)|^2] \leq M$ for all t on $[t_0,T]$ and arbitrary M

(4) $\int_{t_0}^{T} E[|x(t)|^2]dt < \infty$

(5) $x(t) - x(t_0)$ is independent of the stochastic process $\{d\beta(\tau);\ \tau \geq t\}$ for every t on $[t_0, T]$

(6) The stochastic process $\{x(t),\ t \in [t_0,T]\}$ is a Markov process and, in a mean square sense, is uniquely determined by the initial condition $x(t_0)$.

We now consider theorems to a stochastic calculus which will allow integration of stochastic differential equations. These will be used in Chapter V and are included here to complete this appendix.

Theorem: Ito's Differential Rule

Let $x(t)$ satisfy the stochastic differential equation

$$dx = f(x,t)dt + g(x,t)d\beta$$

where $\beta(t)$ is a Wiener-Levy process. f and g are assumed independent of future Brownian motion, with $E(|d\beta(t)|^2) = q(t)dt$. Let $F(x,t)$ be a continuous function in x and t with continuous partial derivatives $\partial F/\partial x$ and $\partial F/\partial t$. Consider the function $y = F(x,t)$. The stochastic differential equation of y is

$$dF = \frac{\partial F}{\partial t}dt + \frac{\partial F}{\partial x}dx + \frac{1}{2}g^2(x,t)q(t)\frac{\partial^2 F}{\partial x^2}dt$$

or

$$dF = \left(\frac{\partial F}{\partial t} + \frac{\partial F}{\partial x}f(x,t) + \frac{1}{2}g^2(x,t)q(t)\frac{\partial^2 F}{\partial x^2}\right)dt + \frac{\partial F}{\partial x}g(x,t)d\beta$$

For vector stochastic processes, it can be shown that if x and f are n-vectors, g is an n.m. matrix, and β is an m-vector Brownian motion process with $E(d\beta(t)d\beta(t)) = Q(t)dt$. Then,

$$dF = \frac{\partial F}{\partial t} dt + \frac{\partial F'}{\partial x} dx + \frac{1}{2} \text{trace } gQg' \frac{\partial^2 F}{\partial x^2} dt$$

where

$$\partial F/\partial t = \partial F/\partial t, \quad \partial F'/\partial x = [\partial F/\partial x_1, \ldots, \partial F/\partial x_n]$$

and

$$\frac{\partial^2 F}{\partial x^2} = \begin{vmatrix} \frac{\partial^2 F}{\partial x^2} & \cdots & \frac{\partial^2 F}{\partial x_1 \partial x_n} \\ \vdots & & \vdots \\ \frac{\partial^2 F}{\partial x_n \partial x_1} & \cdots & \frac{\partial^2 F}{\partial x_n^2} \end{vmatrix} \partial x_n$$

<u>Corollaries</u>

(1) Let $F(x)$ be a twice continuously differentiable real scalar function of the real variable x. Let $G(x) = \partial F/\partial x$ and consider the process $\{\beta(t), t \geq t_0\}$ with variance σ^2. Then for $t_0 < T$

$$\int_{t_0}^{T} G(\beta) d\beta = F(\beta(T)) - F(\beta(t_0)) - \int_{t_0}^{T} \frac{\partial^2 F}{\partial x^2} (\beta) \sigma^2 dt$$

(2) Consider two scalar functions $F(x,t)$ and $G(y,t)$ satisfying the assumptions of Ito's differential rule. Let $H = FG$ be the product of these two functions; then the stochastic differential equation of the product is given by; $d(FG) = GdF + FdG + g^2 q \frac{\partial F}{\partial x} \frac{\partial F}{\partial y} dt$

(3) Let $G(y,t) > 0$ and let $F(x,t)$, $G(y,t)$ satisfy the assumptions of Ito's differential rule. Then the quotient F/G has a stochastic differential equation given by:

$$d(F/G) = (1/G)dF - (F/G^2)dG - (g^2 q \frac{\partial F}{\partial x} \frac{\partial G}{\partial y}/G^2)dt + (Fg^2 q \frac{\partial F}{\partial x} \frac{\partial G}{\partial y}/G^3)dt.$$

PART II: Decision Making - Over Time

> The formulation of a problem is often more essential than its solution which may merely be a matter of mathematical or experimental skill.
>
> Albert Einstein

CHAPTER III: Planning Decisions-- Over Time

III.1 Introduction

In the first part of this book time, temporal problems, and those properties of time relevant to modeling were investigated. In this and the next chapter we shall use the systems approach in dealing with the notions and applications of decision making in time.

Systems theory consists of defining those terms, notions, and structures which have an application to a variety of fields. The most general definition of system is a set of interacting units with relationships among them.[1] Although a more precise and encompassing definition of what systems are is difficult, they are usually applied and used with far greater ease. For example, system theory is applied by a general when he maps his strategy as a sequence of steps, moves and countermoves on the battlefield. A captain steering his boat at sea has a system of variables such as current flow, wind velocity, coordinates, etc., helping him to identify the best route to follow. A firm adopting a particular structural configuration and implementing communication and decision making procedures is also a system. In this chapter we shall provide an approach for the modeling of decision making systems over time or control. We will distinguish between three forms of control: (1) Input control, (2) Transformation process control and (3) Output control. Each of these control modes gives rise to a variety of problems, function of the type of influence that may be exerted on a system's time path. These influences may be:

(i) Internally motivated stimuli, in which case the system is said to be controlled.[2]

(ii) Externally motivated stimuli, in which case the system is said to be supervised.[3]

(iii) External disturbances, in which case the system is said to be disturbed. If the disturbances are probabilistic we say that the system operates in an uncertain (or stochastic) environment.

The managerial quest for better and more desirable system trajectories is also reflected in these three elements. Thus, by better decision making procedures and control actions, managers achieve correspondingly better time paths. The search for *best* time paths, found by application of optimization methods in terms of one or more criteria is called optimal control. The choice of optimal control strategies will be discussed in Chapters IV and V.

III. 2 Control Systems- Over Time

The control of systems over time consists in determining decision making strategies which can manipulate a system's behavior for some desired end. This class of problems is extremely important in management since many studies are concerned with devising desirable characteristics of control mechanisms. Over time, the dependence of events and the carry-over effects of current decisions upon future states prescribe that greater attention be given to:

The design of control systems which can act on the basis of a systems history and the anticipation of future states.

The implications and implementation of control
decisions as they relate to both the managerial
mode and costs inherent in making decisions.

The investigation of long-term effects, stability
and sensitivity of a decision making strategy.

In the static domain, a decision's effect is registered and traced instantaneously in the framework of a model. Over time, however, a decision has implications for future states as well as future decision making flexibility available to the manager. The allocation or resources in the present is in effect a commitment for the future. As a result, over time, managerial actions are influenced by the past history (memory) of the processes they (the managers) control, the additional information they can generate, and the anticipation of the effects their decisions will have on future states. The design of control systems whose sole purpose is the elaboration of decision making strategies consists then in evaluating that strategy which best conforms to managerial measures of effectiveness. By best, we indicate the existence of a scale comparing and evaluating alternative paths and ordering the desirability of these paths. The design of such control systems is therefore a procedure for evaluating the decision strategies which result in the best time paths. For example, assume that a production manager is to devise a production schedule. On the basis of which criteria is this production schedule determined? Typically, the manager will investigate the effects his production schedule has on inventory, using demand forecasts. Given such expected time paths of inventory, he can schedule the production plan by determining an appropriate measure of production and inventory cost.

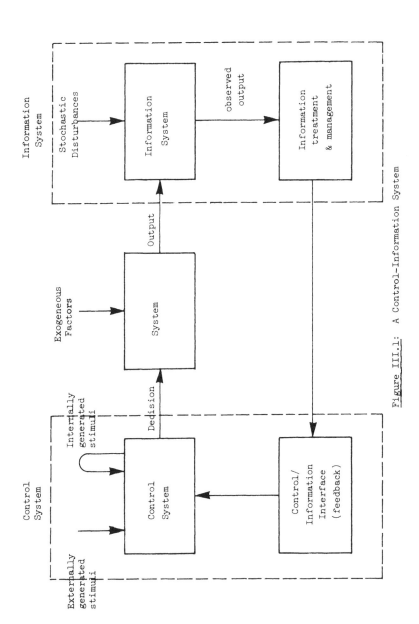

Figure III.1: A Control-Information System

To reach the best design, however, the manager needs to formulate his problem in a way which can lead, after appropriate mathematical manipulations, to the best solution. To a great extent, the systems approach provides a framework amenable to quantitative modeling and resolution.

Associated with and prior to the determination of appropriate control strategies are the problems of implementation and design of information systems which can support the implementation of decision strategies. The design of control systems often becomes a useless exercise if it does not consider problems of:

> Timely availability of information
>
> Costs of searching, gathering, processing and sending information to decision makers
>
> Limitations on decision making complexity and acceptable managerial practices.

For example, the implementation of a best inventory control policy becomes unfeasible if one cannot maintain records of inventory. In general, therefore, in conjunction with the design of control systems are problems concerned with the design of information systems. This topic will be investigated in Chapter V and we note there that operational control is exercised on both control and information systems. The interdependence between control and information systems requires that both systems be closely related and coordinated, as is described in Figure III.1.

In the control problems to be outlined, we will allude to
disturbances, control variables and state variables. Disturbances
are known or probabilistically known (or unknown) time functions
which affect the system behavior. Control variables are variables
which may be manipulated by the manager. And, state
variables are introduced to parametrize the set of input-output
pairs in such a way as to achieve a unique dependence of the
output on input and state. Since there are many ways in which
a set of input-output pairs can be parametrized, the implication
is that there are many ways in which an input-output relation can
be cast into the form of an input-output-state relation. In other
words, state variables in systems are defined entirely by the model
constructed by the analyst. The definition of state
variable is thus applicable only with respect to specific models.

Finally, the manager may establish designs of control
systems not only on the basis of measures of effectiveness but
also on the basis of the stability and the sensitivity of a
system's trajectories. This is particularly the case if the
managerial planning time is very large, and if measures of
effectiveness are difficult to find. In such circumstances,
"design" consists in selecting decision strategies which will
respond to system disturbances in such a way as to return the
system's time path to a specified time trajectory. While there
may be many stabilizing decision strategies, managerial choice
of strategies can be based on decision strategies having a

predescribed degree of stability: that is, strategies which can make the system's time path a stable one following a prescribed speed. The class of problems indicated have to do not only with government policies and macro-economics, but with any system linearized about a desired trajectory as well. The effectiveness of such policies can, for example, be measured in terms of their response time.

The sensitivity of a time-dependent trajectory is again an important element in managerial design of control systems. Typically, models are a poor representation of reality, and although model parameters are assumed known for convenience, in practice there is much uncertainty concerning the value of these parameters. As a result, if a decision strategy (found on the assumption of certain model parameters "a") leads to some measure of effectiveness A and to a time path x_a, it is of considerable practical importance to investigate what that performance and time path turn out to be if, instead of "a", the model parameters were "a+ Δa". If the parameter change Δa matters little, we say that the system is insensitive, and vice versa. Unless there is some design cost of achieving insensitivity, it would always pay to have it.

While we have thus far discussed the notion of control and design of control systems we have not as yet indicated what it is that we wish to control. We will next consider three classes of controls each giving rise to a variety of interesting problems.

(i) Input Control - for example, decision making can be considered as the design of inputs which are selected in order to affect a process.

(ii) Transformation Process Control - for example, the choice of production techniques can be thought of as the design of transformation processes. Similarly, design of a feedback decision mechanism can be considered as a transformation process, albeit of a different type.

(iii) Output Control - for example, the choice of estimates and indicators in an information system may be considered as resulting from the design of outputs.

Input Control (see Figure III.2) gives rise to several special control problems, distinguished by the existence (or) non-existence) of probabilistic disturbances. When there are no disturbances, the control is called deterministic control; otherwise it is called stochastic control. The tools used to resolve problems of a deterministic and stochastic nature are essentially different. In this book, we shall limit ourselves by developing methods for converting stochastic control into deterministic control problems. As a result, the analytical tools required for the design of inputs are greatly simplified.

Transformation process control (see Figure III.3) gives rise to two classes of control problems: identification and configuration control. Identification is concerned with the selection of structures and parameters which "best" fit our knowledge of the system behavior.

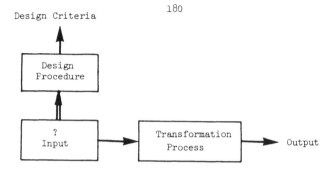

Figure III.2: Input Control

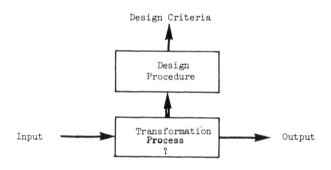

Figure III.3: Transformation Process Control

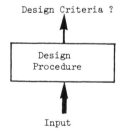

Figure III.4: Inverse Control and Output Control

Configuration control, on the other hand, is concerned with the design of parameters and structures which are best according to the design criteria. Although both problems are of a similar nature, their purpose and use are very different. While identification problems are considered whenever managers wish to reduce the uncertainty of their transformation processes, configuration control problems are considered when the decision processes are limited to prespecified structures.

A combination of input-transformation process controls may also yield a variety of other problems known as adaptive control problems. These problems are characterized by uncertainty concerning the transformation processes, and manipulation of some of the inputs.

Finally, in output control, (see Figure III.4 and III.5), we consider two different types of problems: inverse control and estimation. Inverse control consists in selecting the criteria whose optimization leads to a particular input. That is, it is the reverse of the input control problem determined earlier. Estimation, on the other hand, consists in selecting the output estimates of an information system whose input is data with possible prior knowledge of the estimates. As Figure III.4 indicates, estimation is both an input control with respect to the design procedure of the estimates and an output control with respect to the information system.

Each of the control problems we have outlined indicates a degree of knowledge (or lack of it) of the system parameters, functions, and structures. The effective quantitative resolution of such control problems requires that first these be framed in a quantitative format

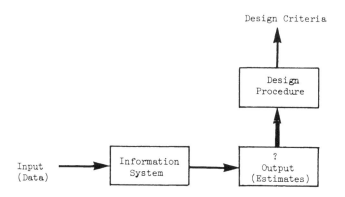

Figure III.5: Estimation and Output Control

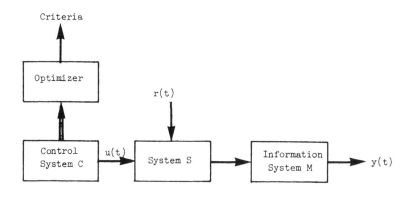

Figure III.6: Deterministic Control

recognized as solvable within the limits of known analytical, numerical or simulation theories. Such quantification will be reached below.

For simplification, we will assume that the greek letters indicate stochastic disturbances, "C" are decision systems, "S" are the transformation processes, and "M" denote information systems. Thus, if S transforms u into x, we will write xSu.

(1) Deterministic Control Problems

Assume that C is a control system or manager making decisions $u(t)$ at time t. These decisions together with environmental variables $r(t)$ at t will determine a state $x(t)$ at t of the system. Our observation of the system is, however, not $x(t)$ but some variable $y(t)$. This variable is observed through an information system which for the moment does not contain sources of uncertainty. Consider the following Figure III.6. The problem of deterministic control is:

<u>Given</u>: The functional relationships (dynamic or not) between
$u(t)$, $x(t)$, $r(t)$, $y(t)$:

xS(u,r,t) at t

<u>Find</u>: The control mechanism C yielding decisions $u(t)$ such that the state $x(t)$ or its observation $y(t)$ is more "to our liking."

By "our liking" is meant optimization with respect to criteria of performance as indicated in Chapter I, as well as acceptable system and state stability and sensitivity. The general optimum deterministic control problem would include all these operational dimensions. In addition, S & M may or may not be given as explicit functions of time, and $x(t)$ & $u(t)$ may or may not be constrained.

Since r(t) is known, a choice of u(t) will determine x(t) by S while x(t) will determine y(t) by M. If u(t) is an explicit time function, it will be called an open-loop control. If u(t) is an explicit function of y(t), it will be called a closed-loop or feedback control.

Quantative Formulation:

The formulation of the deterministic control problem outlined above did not specify the structure or the properties of S and M. A quantitative formulation requires, however, that both S and M be functionally specified. For demonstration purposes, we shall assume that S describes a relationship between x and u,r,t, by a differential equation, while M describes a relationship between y and x, t by a simple equation. Also, the criteria for design will consist in the cumulative sum of some function L of y,u,r,t to be minimized over a planning time $\pm [0,T]$.

A quantitative formulation of the deterministic control problem is therefore:

Given: the dynamic functional relationships

S: $dx(t)/dt = S(x,u,r,t)$

M: $y = M(x,t)$

Find: u(t) subject to constraints on

$u(t) \in U$

$y(t) \in Y$

which minimize a measure of performance

$$\int_0^T L(y,u,r,t)\, dt$$

Because of the importance of this class of problems in management decision making over time we shall consider several examples. These examples will be solved optimally in the next chapter.

(2) Estimation

When a system is subject to stochastic disturbances, the measurement of states is not without error. In this case, it is necessary to find some estimates of the states which may in turn be used for:

>Observing where we are
>
>Where we can expect to go

For example, a production manager can develop better production schedules if he can have better estimates of future demands (forecasts). Similarly, a social planner is in a position to make "better" decisions if he has some reliable estimates of future population characteristics and trends. Errors and disturbances occur for two essential reasons:

> The model representing the system behavior cannot account for all possible interactions and variables and therefore there is a subset of variables which is lumped together and assumed to have stochastic effects.
>
> The measurement of states is itself subject to errors and disturbances.

The estimation problem consists in selecting estimates of states which will be best in some sense. Figure III.7 summarizes this problem which can be stated as follows:

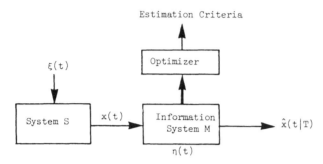

Figure III.7: Estimation

Given:

1. the functional relationship S between $x(t)$ and $\xi(t)$

2. the functional relationship M between $x(t)$, $\eta(t)$ and estimates of $x(t)$

3. a statistical description of the random variables $\xi(t)$, $\eta(t)$

Find: the "best" estimates (in the sense of estimation criteria such as best fit, unbiasedness, consistency, least variance, etc.) of $x(t)$: $\hat{x}(t|T)$ on the basis of measurements of $x(t)$ up to time T.

The estimation problem has three particular cases of interest.

1. Filtering: when t=T, this is called the filtering problem. This amounts to estimating the state of the system on the basis of all past and present observations. In other words, a separation between the values of the states and the stochastic disturbances is attempted.

2. Prediction or Forecasting: when t > T, this is called the prediction or forecasting problem. This amounts to generating estimates for future time periods on the basis of past and current observations of the system. The problem is of immense importance in operations management.

3. Smoothing: when t < T, this is called the smoothing problem. This entails the determination of estimates on the basis of

future observations, and is used for smoothing the system trajectory. While the forecasting problem is used to determine posterior states to the observation time, smoothing is used to determine prior states to the observation time.

The mathematical analysis of the estimation problem is by no means an easy one, and can be reached by several alternative methods. It is worth noting that filtering, forecasting, and smoothing have essentially the same mathematical definitions even though they have radically different implications for the practice of management. Since estimation is commonly associated with information systems, these problems will be investigated in greater detail in Chapter V.

Quantitative Formulation

For a quantitative formulation of the estimation problem, it is convenient to introduce the following notations:

Y^t: is the set of all past observations of a system up to and including time t. That is,

$Y^t = \{y(\tau) \mid \tau \leq t\}$

$\hat{x}(t \mid T)$: is the conditional mean estimate of the state $x(t)$ at time t given a set of observations up to and including time T. That is,

$\hat{x}(t \mid T) = E\{x(t) \mid Y^T\}$

where E is the expectation operator. Also, the least-square estimation error criterion[4] will be used as a "measure of performance" in selecting an estimate of $x(t)$ at time t. The estimation error is given by $\tilde{x}(t|T)$ where

$$\tilde{x}(t|T) = x(t) - \hat{x}(t|T)$$

The expected conditional error (upon the observation set Y^T) is given by:

$$E\{\tilde{x}(t|T)|Y^T\} = \hat{x}(t|T) - \hat{x}(t|T) = 0$$

The expected conditional squared error is, on the other hand, given by the variance $V_{\tilde{x}}$ where

$$V_{\tilde{x}} = E\{\tilde{x}^2(t|T)|Y^T\} = E\{(x(t) - \hat{x}(t|T))^2 | Y^T\}$$

The quantitative estimation problem may thus be formulated as:

Given:

1. The functional relationship S between the state $x(t)$ and the disturbance $\xi(t)$ at time t

   $S: dx(t)/dt = S(x,\xi,t)$

2. The functional relationship between the states $x(t)$ and measurement of the states $y(t)$ with the measurement errors $\eta(t)$ at time t

   $y(t) = M(x,\eta,t)$

3. A statistical description [5] of the random variables ξ, η.

Find:

An estimate $x(t)$; $\hat{x}(t|T)$ based on a data set Y^T

Application of such problems to the estimation of Time Series will be given in Chapter V.

(3) Stochastic Control

When both the systems under investigation and the state measurements are subject to external stochastic disturbances and the manager is still called upon to make decisions, we then have a stochastic control problem. Such problems determine in themselves a whole class of new and difficult problems. The general stochastic control problem involves simultaneously the generation of:

> Optimum estimates and estimation mechanisms
> Optimum decisions and decision mechanisms
> Optimum mechanism for coupling estimates to decision procedures

Figure III.8 describes a stochastic control system where $\xi(t)$ is a system stochastic disturbance, $E(t)$ a deterministic disturbance, and $\eta(t)$ the measurement of the stochastic disturbance. This problem results from coupling estimation to decision models, and involves the simultaneous design of decision and information strategies. The stochastic control problem can be stated as follows:

Given:

1. the functional relationship between $x(t)$, $\xi(t)$, $u(t)$ and $E(t)$; S
2. The statistical description of $\xi(t)$ and $\eta(t)$.

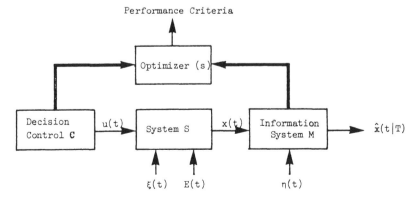

Figure III.8: Stochastic Control Problem

Find simultaneously:

1. a decision strategy u(t) such that some estimates of x(t) $\hat{x}(t \mid T)$ are "more to our liking"

2. an estimation strategy for x(t) such that $\hat{x}(t \mid T)$ is "more to our liking"

If the decision strategy u(t) is a function (known or unknown) of the estimates $\hat{x}(t \mid T)$:

$$u(t) = \{ F \; \hat{x}(\tau) \; \tau \leq T) \}$$

This is called a feedback stochastic control problem.

Simultaneous decision and information strategies design are expectedly difficult. Therefore, a separation of the two problems is often sought. Under these conditions, stochastic control consists in:

1. selecting "best" estimates according to estimation criteria

2. selecting "best" decision **strategies** according to system performance criteria

3. selecting "best" modes for coupling estimates to decisions (the feedback case)

Computationally, stochastic control problems are hard to resolve, For this reason, the choice of probabilistic processes characterizing system and measurement disturbances is extremely important. From the computational point of view, a particularly felicitous situation arises when these processes are chosen in such a way as to allow transformation of the original stochastic control problem into a deterministic equivalent one. One of the major tasks undertaken in the book (see Chapter V) is to determine when such transformations can be performed. Basically, three methods are proposed for effecting these transformations:

(1) approximating the evolution of stochastic processes by the probability parameters of these processes (e.g. finding the mean-variance evolution)

(2) seeking self-reproducing probability processes which will describe functional correspondence between parameters of probability processes - in successive instants of time.

(3) seeking "filtering" methods which will yield the best estimates over time as a function of known current and past observations

When such a "transformation" cannot be reached, analytical tools usually break down, and the remaining best avenue open to the operations manager is simulation techniques, as will be indicated in Chapter VI.

Quantitative Formulation

The stochastic control problem can be formulated quantitatively by combining the deterministic control and estimation problems. Letting greek letters denote random disturbances, we can write:

Given:
1. The functional relationship S between x and u, ξ, r
   $S: dx(t)/dt = S(x,u,r,\xi,t)$
2. The functional relationship M between the measurements y and x, u, η.
   $M: y(t) = M(x,u,\eta,t)$
3. A statistical description of ξ, η.

Find:

u(t) subject to constraints on: $u(t) \in \psi$, or $u(Y^t) \in \psi$
probability constraints on $x(t)$: $\mathcal{P}\{x(t)\} \in P$
which minimize the expectation (or some other probability
parameter) of the measure of performance, conditional upon
the history Y^t;

$$\int_0^T E\{L(x,u,r,t) \mid Y^t\} dt$$

in a given or not given planning time $[0,T]$

The quantitative solution of stochastic control problems is a difficult one and to date, only special cases have successfully been resolved. For this reason, simulation is a necessary tool for investigating the alternative decision strategies in stochastic control problems.

(4) Identification

Earlier, the transformation of inputs into outputs was achieved by assuming the functional relationship of the system S. This is not always the case, especially in social systems where the impact of decision-effects can rarely be traced (even probabilistically). The problem, then, is to seek methods which, on the basis of inputs and outputs, can indicate how the inputs are transformed into our observation of system states. This class of problems is known as identification problems and is represented in Figure III 9. The problem can be stated as follows:

Given:
1. the functional relationship between $y(t)$, $\eta(t)$, and $x(t)$
2. the measurable quantities $\hat{x}(t|T)$ and $u(t)$
3. the statistical descriptions of $\xi(t)$ and $\eta(t)$

Find: a best estimate of the system functional relationship between
$x(t)$ and $u(t)$, $r(t)$, $\xi(t)$.

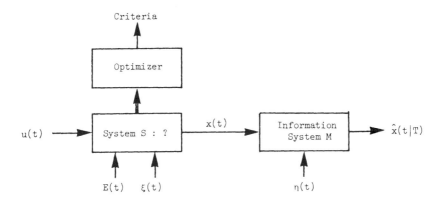

Figure III.9: Identification

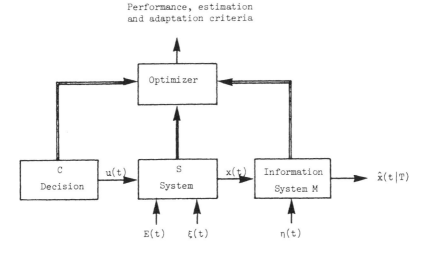

Figure III.10: Adaptive Control

Two approaches can be distinguished in the solution of this complex problem:

1. Design: In this case, identification is achieved by imposing external criteria of best fit, best performance etc., and the functional relationship is designed accordingly. The function of the 'optimizer' is then to incorporate new data adaptively in the design of the system S.

2. Behavioral: In this case, identification is found by methods which are not based on optimizing criteria. The behavioral theory of the firm[6] -- seeking to explain how a set of input resources, personnel and management policies is transformed into products and economic welfare -- is an example in point. The method there is to find likely transformation processes rather than optimum processes.

Quantitative Formulation

Given:

1. The functional relationship S between x, ξ, r, and α where α is a set of unknown parameters.
    S: $dx(t)/dt = S(x,r,\alpha,\xi,t)$

2. The functional relationship M between the measurements y and x, η, α.
    M: $y(t) = M(x,\alpha,\eta,t)$.

3. A statistical description of ξ, η.

Find: Estimates of parameters α given a data set $Y^t = \{y(\tau)|\ \tau \leq t\}$

(5) Adaptive Control

Adaptive control occurs when the manager is required to control an unknown (or partially unknown) process. He is required to identify the process and represent it by a structural form whose parameters are estimated on the basis of system observations. The adaptive control problem is a further generalization of the stochastic control problem as Figure III.10 shows. Here, criteria are used to simultaneously determine the decision and information strategies as well as the system transformation processes.

The adaptive control problem can be stated as follows:

Given:
1. The measurable quantities $\hat{x}(t|T)$ and the given decision $u(t)$
2. The statistical description of $\xi(t)$ and $\eta(t)$

Find Simultaneously
1. A mechanism for generating decisions
2. A model for the system S describing a temporal functional relationship between $x(t)$, $u(t)$, $\xi(t)$ and $\eta(t)$.
3. an information system describing the temporal relationship between $\hat{x}(t|T)$, $x(t)$ and $\eta(t)$.

such that the problem's performance, estimation and adaptive control criteria are "best in some sense".

As pointed out, in the deterministic and stochastic control cases the decisions $u(t)$ can be given as a function of the observed state $\hat{x}(t|T)$.

$$u(t) = F\{\hat{x}(t|T)\}$$

This will be called the closed-loop adaptive control problem.

Adaptive control problems are difficult to solve and have large memory requirements. Mechanisms designed to learn about the system S on the basis of new information are also complex. These problems are, very important, however, as they can provide rational bases for the modeling and operation of complex social systems.

(6) Inverse Control

In the previous sections a managerial rationality, expressed by a set of performance, estimation and adaptation criteria, was postulated. Given such a rationality, the control problem was defined by the selection of strategies, considered best in light of the managerial rationality. Inverse control consists in determining what criteria are optimized (if any) by the choice of a particular control strategy.

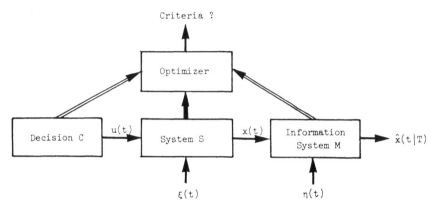

Figure III.11: Inverse Control

The inverse control problem is what Churchman[7] called the problem of rationality, i.e., determine criteria of behavior given the rules of behavior. This problem can be stated as follows:

Given:
1. a functional description between a system's input actions $u(t)$, disturbances $\xi(t)$ and states $x(t)$
2. observable and estimated states $\hat{x}(t|T)$ as well as input actions $u(t)$
3. a functional description between states $x(t)$, estimates $\hat{x}(t|T)$ and measurement errors $\eta(t)$
4. statistical description of $\xi(t)$ and $\eta(t)$

Find: the criteria (if any) which are optimized by a decision strategy $u(t)$.

The inverse control problem has received little attention compared to other problems. It may be useful, however, in determining the stability of a particular decision program and in yielding a systematic definition of those social processes seeking 'economy' and 'efficiency'. This approach has been particularly applicable in physics, and many physical phenomena have been explained by the discovery of such efficiency criteria. Notable examples are: Fermat's Principle of Least Time, Maupertius' Principle of Least Action, Hamilton's Principle, Plateau's Problem, etc. In biology, Darwin suggested a principle of natural selection based on survival of the fittest, Rashevsky,[8] inverting the problem, suggested a principle of optimal design:

> Biological structures which are optimal in
> the context of natural selection, are also
> optimal in the sense that they minimize
> some cost functional derived from the
> engineering characteristics of the situation.

Similarly, in social and economic systems, we can postulate the existence of principles of optimality. To determine these principles, however, the social transformation processes must be identified and the temporal evolution of a social system's variables must be observed. In other words, by stating that every social and/or economic state is optimal in some sense, and by making temporal observations of system states and managerial actions, the optimality criteria, drawn from the characteristics of the model, can theoretically be defined. This approach, described in Figure III.11 is an inverse control problem.

Quantitative Formulation

The general quantitative formulation of the inverse control

problem can be stated by following Figure III.11 and by postulating the appropriate mathematical relationships between inputs and outputs. This formulation would, however, be of little practical use as, to date, very few inverse control problems have been resolved.[9] The deterministic inverse control problem has received some attention and therefore we shall refer to this version of the problem.

Given:

1. The functional relationship between x and u

    S: $dx(t)/dt = S(x,u,t)$

2. The control strategy $u(t)$ (or $u(x,t)$ in feedback form).

Find:

The loss functions $L(x,u,t)$

$$J(T) = \int_0^T L(x,u,t)dt$$

which is minimized by the choice of u.

III.3 Applications

We consider here several applications of the problems defined in section III.2. These problems will be resolved in Chapter IV.

Example III.1: The Arrow-Karlin (AK) Deterministic Production Control Model [4]

The AK model determines the optimal rate of production $u(t)$ in a known time interval $[t_o, T]$ which minimizes the total production costs such that the demands for a product are always satisfied.

The AK model can be formulated as follows:

$$\text{Minimize } J(T) = \int_{t_o}^{T} \{C(u(t)) + H(x(t))\}dt$$
$$u(t) \geq 0$$

subject to: (3.1)

$$x(t) = x(t_o) + \int_{t_o}^{t} u(\tau)d\tau - \int_{t_o}^{t} s(\tau)d\tau \geq 0$$

where

x(t); inventory on hand at time t

u(t); production rate at time t

C(u(t)); production rate cost at time t

H(x(t)); inventory holding cost at time t

The cost function $C(u(t))$ is assumed twice differentiable and

$$\partial C/\partial u > 0, \quad \partial^2 C/\partial u^2 > 0 \quad (3.2)$$

while $H(x(t))$ is a differentiable increasing function of the inventory $x(t)$.

Now assume that a production changeover cost is added to the production cost function J(T) above. Let this cost be given by $G(du(t)/dt)$, where $du(t)/dt$ is the rate of change in production rate. The production problem may then be formulated as follows:

$$\text{Minimize } J(T) = \int_{t_o}^{T} \{C(u(t)) + G(v(t)) + H(x(t))\} dt$$
$$v(t) \in \Omega$$

subject to: (3.3)

$$x(t) = x(t_o) + \int_{t_o}^{t} u(\tau)d\tau - \int_{t_o}^{t} s(\tau)d\tau \geq 0$$

$$u(t) = u(t_o) + \int_{t_o}^{t} v(\tau)d\tau \geq 0$$

In certain production problems, the production changeover cost is particularly important and each time a production change is reached, a known fixed cost G is incurred. In other words;

$$G(v(t)) = \begin{cases} G & \text{if } du(t)/dt \neq 0 \\ 0 & \text{if } du(t)/dt = 0 \end{cases} \quad (3.4)$$

For the answer to such problems, we can resolve an impulsive control problem, i.e. a problem where decisions are triggered by impulse functions. Alternatively, we may <u>discretise</u> the optimization problem. Consider the latter case and define $t_1, t_2, \ldots \ldots t_{n-1}$ with $t_n = T$ as a set of <u>decision times</u>. Thus,

$$u(t) = u_{j-1} \qquad t_{j-1} \leq t < t_j \quad (3.5)$$
$$v(t_j) = u_j - u_{j-1}$$
$$j = 1, 2, \ldots \ldots n$$

Such a production decision rule is called a <u>step-production decision function</u>. The optimum step-production decision function can then be formulated as one optimizing the production system subject to the added restrictions imposed on $u(t)$ and the cost $G(v(t))$.

<u>Example III.2</u>: Optimum Maintenance and Replacement of Machines: Deterministic Control

In chapter II, the maintenance and deterioration of pieces of equipment were described as memory processes. Given a decision criterion we may now be in a position to formulate a control problem for the design of equipment maintenance strategies and compute the optimum retirement times of machines.

A general statement of the replacement problem could be made as follows: given a machine which will yield a stream of anticipated revenues in time and which has a stream of operating costs in time, in addition to some salvage value at some time t in the future. The problem is then to maximize the present value of this machine, with the present value equal to the discounted values of the revenues plus salvage value minus the operating costs. Applying a control terminology to this problem, the stream of revenues and the salvage value can be looked upon as <u>state variables</u> or states reached indirectly through management intervention. On the other hand, operating costs are <u>control variables,</u> meaning under direct management control. We see the dynamic characteristics of the problem in this formulation; all the variables are functions of time and, in general, future events. It is obvious that a dynamic solution to this problem would yield more realistic results than the static solutions which have been relied upon in the past.

The problem may now be stated:

Maximize $V(T)$

$$V(T) = S(T) e^{-rT} + \int_0^T Q(t) e^{-rt} dt$$

subject to:

$$0 \leq m(t) \leq M$$

$$dS/dt = -D(t) + f(t)m(t) \qquad S(0) = K \qquad (3.6)$$

where $Q(t)$ = revenues - costs and K is the cost of the machine,

$$Q(t) = p(t)S(t) - m(t)$$

This is a deterministic control problem with a linear profit function. An extension of this problem would replace $Q(T)$ - the net revenues of the machine, by:

$Q(t) = p(S,t)S(t)-m(t)$, where the profit rate per $ salvage value is no longer independent of S, but a function of it. We may also consider nonlinear maintenance cost, and refine the definition of maintenance effectiveness. The usefulness of such extensions depends on the characteristics of the maintenance problem at hand.

In practice, businessmen's calculations to retire machines are not only based on the ability of the machine to contribute to profits but also on the competitive value of new and future machines. Thus the decision to replace one machine by another is based on the opportunity costs of not buying the new machines. When it is worthwhile to replace one machine by another, we say that the machine is technically obsolete. The technical obsolescence of a machine refers to a particular machine's production process. For example, planes assigned to passenger transportation may, after the appearance of a new plane, be assigned to freight transportation. Although the first plane is not retired, it is merely working on another production process with different characteristics. Replacement of a machine by another therefore involves two machines rather than one as defined earlier. To extend the analysis, we consider a set of machines bought in sequence. The value of these machines equals the present value of the first machine bought initially at time t_o and retired at t_1, etc., for all subsequent machines subscripted $i, i=1,\ldots n$. Each of the machines has a cost K_1 and discount rate r_i in intervals (t_{i-1}, t_i). Such a problem can be stated as follows: Find the maintenance policies $m_i(t)$, $i=1,\ldots n$ and retirement dates t_i, $i=1,\ldots n$ which maximize the discounted values of the machines.

If we define a variable $k_i(t, t_i)$ as

$$k_i(t, t_i) = \begin{cases} 1 & \text{for } t_{i-1} \leq t < t_i \\ 0 & \text{elsewhere} \end{cases}$$

A quantitative formulation of the problem is as follows:

$$\underset{m_i, t_i}{\text{Maximize}} \quad V(t_n) = \int_{t_o}^{t_n} \sum_{i=1}^{n} [Q_i(t) + \dot{S}_i(t) - r_i S_i(t)] e^{-r_i t} k_i(t, t_i) dt$$

Subject to:

$$\dot{S}_i(t) = [-D_i(t-t_{i-1}) + f_i(t-t_{i-1}) m_i(t-r_{i-1})] k_i(t, t_i)$$

$$0 < m(t-t_i) < M_i \qquad (3.7)$$

$$Q_i(t) = P_i(t) S_i(t) - m_i(t-t_{i-1})$$

Example III.3: Multi-Commodities Transportation Over Time:
Deterministic Control

We reconsider here a multi-commodity version of example II.4 in far greater detail. The variables are defined below and the state equations are derived again.

   a.   The variables

   x_{ij}: Total commodities transported at time t from source i to sink j (n.m. matrix).
   y_{ik}: Inventory of commodity k at source i at time t (n.r matrix).
   z_{jk}: Inventory of commodity k at sink j at time t (m.r. matrix).
   v_{ijk}: Amounts of commodity k transported from source i to sink j at time t (n.m.r. matrix).
   D_{ij}: Total quantities to be transported from source i to sink j (n.m matrix).
   A_{ik}: Total quantities of commodity k to be transported from source i (n.r matrix).
   B_{jk}: Total quantities of commodity k to be shipped to sink j (m.r matrix).
   c_{ij}: Route's capacity between source i and sink j (n.m matrix).
   C: Transportation capability or total transportation capacity.
   α_k: Index expressing capacity per unit required by commodity k when travelling on some route ij (r vector).
   τ_{ijk}: Time or delay required for commodity k, leaving source i, to reach sink j (n.m.r matrix).
   L: A loss functional expressing total cost or performance.
   T: The planning horizon.

   b: The-State Equations

The equations characterizing the system behavior are basically "rate of flows" equations with time delays expressing the time required for commodity k to reach its destination. At time t, the rate of change in total commodity transport is given by:

$$\dot{x}_{ij} = \sum_{k=1}^{r} v_{ijk}(t) \qquad x_{ij}(0)=0 \qquad x_{ij}(T-\min_k \tau_{ijk}) = D_{ij}$$
$$i=1\ldots n; \qquad j=1\ldots m$$

where the initial and final time conditions are assumed known. The inventory of commodity k in source i and sink j are similarly given by:

$$\dot{y}_{ik} = - \sum_{j=1}^{m} v_{ijk}(t) \qquad y_{ik}(0) = A_{ik} \quad y_{ik}(T - \min_j \tau_{ijk}) = 0$$
$$i=1\ldots n;\ k=1\ldots r$$

$$\dot{z}_{jk} = \sum_{i=1}^{n} v_{ijk}(t - \tau_{ijk}) \qquad z_{jk}(0) = 0 \quad z_{jk}(T) = B_{jk}$$
$$j=1\ldots m;\quad k=1\ldots r$$

Also for controllability we require [10]

$$\sum_{i}^{n} A_{ik} = \sum_{j}^{m} B_{jk}; \quad \sum_{k}^{r} A_{ik} = \sum_{j}^{m} D_{ij}; \quad \sum_{k}^{r} B_{jk} = \sum_{i}^{n} D_{ij}$$

The routes' capacity constraints as well as the transportation capacity are given by:

$$0 \leq \sum_{k}^{r} \alpha_k v_{ijk} \leq c_{ij}$$

$$\sum_{i}^{n} \sum_{j}^{n} \sum_{k}^{r} \alpha_k v_{ijk} \leq C$$

Consider a certain quantity v_{ijk} of commodity k being shipped on route ij. The volume per unit of such a commodity is given by $\alpha_k v_{ijk}$. The total commodities transported at any instant of time t on a route ij cannot together have a capacity larger than c_{ij}. Similarly, the total quantity transported cannot exceed our transportation capacity C.

The costs incurred in such a transportation system will, for the moment, consist of a general loss functional whose components are the inventories at the n sources and m sinks as well as the transportation costs. The multi-commodity transportation problem over time may then simply be written as: Minimize

$$J = \int_0^T L(v_{ijk}, y_{ik}, z_{jk}, t) dt$$

$$i=1...n, \; j=1,...m, \; k=1,...r$$

subject to the equations above.

In this formulation we do not clearly distinguish between state and output variables. For this reason, we shall formulate an equivalent problem by introducing a variable η_{ijk}. This variable expresses the 'ij' route utilization of commodity k. η_{ijk} will be defined as a *state* variable, while the transport *control* is to be v_{ijk}. Then an equivalent problem to the one defined by above is to minimize:

$$J = \int_0^T L(v_{ijk}, \eta_{ijk}, \eta_{ijk}(t-\tau_{ijk})) \, dt \qquad (3.8)$$

subject to:

$$\dot{\eta}_{ijk} = v_{ijk} \qquad \eta_{ijk}(0) = 0 \qquad t \in [-\tau_{ijk}, 0] \qquad \forall i,j,k$$

and final conditions

$$\sum_{j}^{m} \eta_{ijk}(T-\tau_{ijk}) = A_{ik} \qquad i=1,...n, \; k=1...r$$

$$\sum_{i}^{n} \eta_{ijk}(T-\tau_{ijk}) = B_{jk} \qquad j=1...m, \; k=1...r$$

$$\sum_{k}^{r} \eta_{ijk}(T-\tau_{ijk}) = D_{ij} \qquad i=1...n, \; j=1...m$$

and

$$0 \leq \sum_{k}^{r} \alpha_k v_{ijk} \leq c_{ij} \qquad i=1,...n, \; j=1...m$$

$$\sum_{i}^{n} \sum_{j}^{m} \sum_{k}^{r} \alpha_k v_{ijk} \leq C$$

To prove the equivalence of these two problems we use the relationships:

$$Y_{ik} = A_{ik} - \sum_{j}^{m} \eta_{ijk}$$

$$z_{jk} = \sum_{i}^{n} \eta_{ijk}(t - \tau_{ijk})$$

$$x_{ij} = \sum_{k}^{r} \eta_{ijk}$$

Using these equations and substituting them wherever appropriate, we obtain the same problem. Furthermore, by computing the final time of y_{ik}, z_{jk}, and x_{ij} in terms of η_{ijk} we obtain the final time conditions. This formulation of the problem is far more concise and will lead to results that are mathematically tractable. Here η_{ijk} is a state variable while v_{ijk} is the control variable. The state variable appears in the cost functional with time delays τ_{ijk}.

Applications such as Minimum Time Transportation, linear inventory, and transportation costs, implying specific functional forms, will be investigated in Chapter IV.

Example III.4   Time Variable and Stochastic Demand Production Models

In this example, a general stochastic problem is formulated. Thereafter, special cases are indicated. The production-inventory equation is given by:

$$x_{t+1} = x_t + u_t - s_t$$

where x_t is the inventory on hand at time t and u_t the production rate at time t.

Let s_t --the demand, be probabilistic and be defined by:

$$s_{t+1} = f(s_t, a_t, \xi_{1t})$$
$$a_{t+1} = g(a_t, \xi_{2t})$$

where s_t is the demand at time t, function of the slope a(t) and a random function ξ_{1t} which we assume to be a standard Wiener process. The slope a_t also evolves randomly with a standard Wiener process ξ_{2t}. Measurements of the demand is given by time series concerning the demand and the slope a_t. Let Z^t and A^t be these time series. That is, if:

$$y_{1t} = s_t + \eta_{1t}$$
$$y_{2t} = a_t + \eta_{2t}$$

where η_{1t} and η_{2t} are two uncorrelated random functions of time.

Then,

$$Z^t = \{ y_{1t} \mid \tau = 0, 1, \ldots t\}$$
$$A^t = \{ y_{2t} \mid \tau = 0, 1, \ldots t\}$$

These time series provide the data required to establish forecasts of demand, and inventory on hand, and establish production plans. The criteria for establishing production plans are different from these encountered in inventory models. While in inventory models "production" costs are essentially fixed costs, in production these may (in the case of production set-ups) or may not involve a fixed cost. Since production plans can be reached at each time period on the basis of past performance and observations, shifting and on-line production plans can be defined and updated as new data is acquired. Several problems of estimation, (filtering, forecasting) identification and stochastic control occurring in production control will be defined.

Define by L_T the terminal, total production cost. Given the following costs;

$L_1(x_t) =$ inventory cost at time t.
$L_2(u_t) =$ production cost at time t.
$L_3(v_t) =$ production change-over cost at time t.

The following stochastic production problem can be formulated.

Minimize $E \{L_T \mid z^t, A^t, T > t\}$ (3.9)

subject to:

$$L_T = [\sum_{t=0}^{T} L_1(x_t) + L_2(u_t) + L_3(v_t)]$$

$x_{t+1} = x_t + u_t - s_t; \quad E(x_0) = x^0, \quad var(x_0) = 0$

$u_{t+1} = u_t + v_t; \quad u_0 = u^0$

$s_{t+1} = f(s_t, a_t, \xi_{1t}); \quad E(s_0) = s^0, \quad var(s_0) = \sigma_{10}^2$

$a_{t+1} = g(a_t, \xi_{2t}); \quad E\{a_0\} = a^0, \quad var\{a^0\} \sigma_{20}^2$

$y_{1t} = s_t + n_{1t}$

$y_{2t} = a_t + n_{2t}$

$z^t = \{y_{1\tau} \mid \tau = 0,1,\ldots t\}$

$A^t = \{y_{2\tau} \mid \tau = 0,1,\ldots t\}$

and the following constraints :

$\alpha_1(x_t) \quad \varepsilon\Omega_1$: Inventory constraints

$\alpha_2(u_t) \quad \varepsilon\Omega_2$: Production constraints

$\alpha_3(v(t)) \quad \varepsilon \Omega_3$: Production changeover constraints where $E\{ \cdot \}$ is the expectation operator of probability theory.

This formulation of the production problem is a very general one and need not be considered as one problem but several dependent problems. We define these problems next.

(1) Estimation-Demand is an uncontrolled input to production management (although in certain economic conditions such as monopoly, it can be partially controlled). For this reason, it is important that we establish forecasts of demand and use these in reaching production decisions. The demand estimation problem consists in establishing conditional estimates $\hat{s}$ and $\hat{a}$ on the basis of the time series Z and A. Namely, find;

$$\hat{s}_{t|\tau} = E\{s_t | Z^\tau, A^\tau\}$$
$$\hat{a}_t = E\{a_t | Z^\tau, A^\tau\}$$

which is best in the sense of a decision criterion. Compare t and τ, the time reference for the demand estimate and τ, the the time series. Then;

$\quad\quad$ t = τ : Demand Filtering

$\quad\quad$ t > τ : Demand Forecasting

Let ε_{1t} and ε_{2t} be error forecasts for example :

$$\varepsilon_{1t} = s_t - \hat{s}_{t|\tau}$$
$$\varepsilon_{2t} = a_t - \hat{a}_{t|\tau}$$

A criterion for choosing estimates to which we shall return in Chapter V consists in minimizing the squared errors. Such estimates are called least squares estimates. If the errors are weighted as a function of their point of reference in time (e.g. recent observations weighing more than older ones) we obtain weighted least square estimates.

(ii) Identification-- Assume that the demand process is given by:
$$s_{t+1} = f(s_t, a, \xi_t)$$
$$y_{1t} = s_t + \eta_{1t}$$

where a, a slope, is an unknown random variable. Then, estimation of the demand (i.e., its forecast) entails an estimation of the parameter $\hat{a}$ as well. This defines an identification problem and involves simultaneous estimation of the state s_t of the demand process and the parameter $\hat{a}$ specifying (together with the function f) the process' evolution.

(iii) Production Smoothing-- Let the data set $\{Z^\tau, A^\tau\}$ where $\tau > T$ be given. This data is then used to establish production decisions in the time interval [0,T]. That is, the production criterion defined by (.) is reformulated as:

$$\underset{v_t, t=0,1,\ldots T}{\text{Minimize}} \; E \{L_T \mid Z^t, A^t, \tau > T\}$$

Minimization of (iii) subject to (ii) - (i) is a production smoothing problem in that future outcomes are used to determine what production decisions are to be reached on the basis of a time series longer than the plan. This is described graphically in Figure III. 13. We shall return to a solution of such problems in Chapter V.

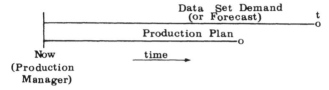

Figure III.12

<u>Example III.6</u> Estimation and Control of Probabilistic

Proportional Effects through Time Series

In many examples of management science, it is difficult, and often impossible to find the equations describing the process of change. That is, the difference or differential equations used to describe how the states of a system evolve in time is not known. Instead a simplistic and probabilistic cause-effect relationship is established between a certain set of actions and their resultant effects. Each action and effect is then recorded over time. The record--i.e. time series-- may be used to estimate the probabilistic proportional effects relating one variable to another. For example, some of the relationship we may consider are:

$u(t)$ $\qquad\qquad\qquad\qquad$ $x(t) = \mu u(t)$
Action $\qquad\qquad\qquad\qquad$ Outcome

(1) Advertising $\qquad\longrightarrow$ **Sales or market share**
(2) Money supply under Federal Control $\longrightarrow$ Market interest rate
(3) Number of policemen $\qquad\longrightarrow$ Crime Rate
(4) Number of cars $\qquad\longrightarrow$ Pollution count
(5) Number of cars $\qquad\longrightarrow$ Gasoline demand

Here μ is a variable describing the probabilistic proportional effect of an action $u(t)$ upon its outcome $x(t)$. Let $y(t)$ be the record of $x(t)$. That is:

$$x(t) = \tilde{\mu}u(t)$$
$$y(t) = x(t) + \eta(t) \quad (3.10)$$

where $\tilde{\mu}$ is a random variable with prior mean m and prior variance σ_m^2. $\eta(t)$ is a Wiener process with variance s^2. The problems we address ourselves to are three fold: (1) estimation of x(t) as data y(t) is collected, (2) estimation (identification) of the parameters $\tilde{\mu}$, also as a function of y(t), (3) the choice of an optimum control u(t) for some given criterion. These problems will be resolved in Chapter V.

Example III.7: Optimum Advertising Under Uncertainty-- The
Goodwill Model

We return to Example II.11 and determine an optimum advertising policy. We assume that sales are some twice differentiable function of goodwill and that the profit functional optimized by the firm is:

$$\int_0^\infty e^{-rt} [\pi(p,x,t) - w(a(t))] dt$$

$\partial\pi/\partial p > 0$, $\partial\pi/\partial x > 0$, $\partial^2\pi/\partial x^2 < 0$ where p(t) is the price at time t. Since x, the goodwill at time t, is a random variable, the profit functional is also a random variable. The choice of an advertising policy should therefore reflect both the profit motive and an attitute towards risk. For example, if a firm's utility function is described by some polynomial, an expected utility criterion could be expressed as a function of the moments of goodwill x.

If $\pi(p,x,t)$ is a linear function, an expected value yields an optimization problem equivalent to that of Nerlove and Arrow. Assume that the expected value of $\pi(p,x,t)$ can be described as a function of the price $p(t)$ and the first two probability moments of goodwill $s(t)$ and $v(t)$ respectively. Maximization of expected goodwill is thus reduced to a standard certainty equivalent deterministic optimum control problem with $s(t)$ and $v(t)$ the state variables and $a(t)$ the control. The mathematical optimization problem is stated as follows:

$$\text{Maximize} \quad J(a(.)) = \int_0^\infty e^{-rt}[\pi(p,s,v,t) - w(a(t))]dt$$

subject to:

$$ds(t)/dt = q(a(t)) - mq(t) \qquad (3.11)$$
$$s(o) = s^o$$
$$dv(t)/dt = -q(a(t)) + ms(t) - 2mv(t)$$
$$v(o) = 0$$

where evolutions of $dq(t)/dt$ and $dv(t)/dt$ will be proved in Chapter V.

A similar procedure can be applied to determine the optimum advertising strategy of the diffusion model defined in Example II.10. Specifically, if we consider $[\pi(p,s,v,t) - w(a,t)]$ as the instantaneous profit criterion with s denoting sales, the mathematical optimization problem is stated as follows:

$$\text{Maximize } J(a(.)) = \int_0^\infty e^{-rt}[\pi(p,s,v,t) - w(a,t)]dt$$

Subject to:

$$ds(t)at = -ms(t) + qa(t)(M-s(t)) \qquad (3.12)$$
$$s(o) = s^o$$
$$dv(t)/dt = M\,qa(t) + [m-qa(t)]s(t) - [m + qa(t)]2v(t)$$
$$v(t) = 0$$

Example I V.8: Allocation of effort over time

Problems of allocation of effort over time are concerned with one or all of the following:

> Establishing a sequence for the allocation of effort in time
>
> Determining the timing of that allocation
>
> Selecting the duration of a particular effort

Each of these problems is of considerable practical importance in management, since time is viewed as a resource which is to be carefully and judiciously managed. For example, consider a salesman selling n products to a well-defined clientele. How much effort (i.e. how much of his own time) should he allocate to selling specific products? When should he do so? These are complex questions; to answer them we must model the effects of sales effort on realized sales. Furthermore, since a sales effort made at one time is carried over to future time periods, we must trace the effects of past effort on current sales (i.e. the memory mechanism). Given a model which includes the effects of sales efforts, the salesman can better allocate his time in selling his n products.

The discussion will now be extended to include essential time-related activities such as:

(1) The carry-over of a salesman's effort from the point at which it is expended to later points in time. Carry-over effects are inherently temporal.

(2) The formation of expectations by salesmen and by their firms. Expectations are formed on the basis of "memory"

of past events

(3) The sequentiality of the decisions allocating sales effort over time, in contrast to models allocating "proportions" of time simultaneously.

Table III.1 shows these three elements contrasted in static and dynamic formulations. The dynamic formultions provide better frameworks than the static ones for realistic planning of sales effort.

STATIC FORMULATION	DYNAMIC FORMULATION
Salesmen have no memory, effect of sales effort is independent of past allocation	Salesmen have memory of past firm's actions rates and quotas, sales are function of past sales effort allocation
Firm does not have memory and does not use sales quotas and commission as a strategic tool for market penetration	Firm has memory and forms expectation of market possibilities and response to sales effort. Uses commissions and quotas as strategic penetration tools
Sales allocation of sales effort to multiple products is simultaneous.	Salesmen allocation of sales effort to multiple product is sequential and based on explicit temporal priorities.

Table III.1: Allocation of Sales Effort -
Static and Dynamic

If sales at t are a function of both current sales efforts and accumulated past efforts, the lagged effects make the problem time-dependent. This time-dependency can be represented by a function $m(t,z)$, so that the effect of sales effort at time z, $u_{ij}(z)$ on sales at t ($t > z$) is $m(t,z)u_{ij}(z)$. The cumulative effect is given by the integral over past periods, so that sales are affected by effort expanded earlier as well as by current effort:

$$u_{ij}(t) = F_{ij}(\tau_{ij}(t))$$
$$q_{ij}(t) = F_{ij}[b_j \int_{-\infty}^{t} m(t,z)u_{ij}(z)dz]$$

where $\tau_{ij}(t)$ = amount of time allocated by salesman i to a product j at time t

$u_{ij}(t)$ = effect of a sales effort $\tau_{ij}(t)$ on willingness to buy the product

$q_{ij}(t)$ = sales of product j by salesman i at time t

For simplicity, we write

$$q_{ij}(t) = b_j \int_{-\infty}^{t} m(t,z)u_{ij}(z)dz$$

where $m(t,z)$ behaves as a weighing function of past efforts. Several density functions can be reasonably considered in empirical applications studying relationships between past prices and current sales. An example is a Gamma probability distribution, or the exponential distribution.

For further development we use an exponential function to weight past sales efforts in terms of their effects on current sales. In the exponential case,

$$q_{ij}(t) = b_j \int_{0}^{t} e^{-m_{ij}(t-z)} u_{ij}(z)dz + q_{ij}(0)e^{-m_j t}$$

can be transformed into

$$\frac{dq_{ij}(t)}{dt} = -m_j q_{ij}(t) + b_j u_{ij}(t)$$

Proceeding with the exponential density function, together with the restriction that salesman j has only a fixed amount of time to allocate to all products:

$$\sum_{i=1}^{n} \tau_{ij}(t) \le 1$$

This results in a system of equations giving realizable sales by allocating effort $\tau_{ij}(t)$:

$$\tau_{ij}(t) \longrightarrow u_{ij}(t) \longrightarrow q_{ij}(t)$$

An allocation of sales effort $\tau_{ij}(t)$ therefore provides a strategy for influencing $u_{ij}(t)$ and sales $q_{ij}(t)$. We consider next the problem of optimum allocation of sales effort.

We define an inverse-sales function as

$$\tau_{ij}(t) = F^{-1}(u_{ij}(t))$$

An optimum sales effort can now be allocated by solving the following optimum control problem:

$$\underset{u_{ij}}{\text{Maximize}} \int_0^T \sum_j^n \sum_i^m p_j q_{ij} - \sum_{j=1}^{n} C_j \left(\sum_{i=1}^{m} q_{ij} \right) e^{-rt} dt$$

subject to:

$$dq_{ij}(t)/dt = -m_i q_{ij} + b_j u_{ij} \qquad q_{ij}(0) = q_{ij}^0$$

$$\sum_{j=1}^{n} F_{ij}^{-1}(u_{ij}) \le 1$$

where F_{ij}^{-1} is the inverse of the sales effectiveness function, p_j are prices of products j, and $C_j(\Sigma q_{ij})$ are the production costs and γ is a discount rate. This is a linear control problem.

III.4 Information Control

In an implicit way, control systems have been assumed to have the appropriate informational base required to reach decisions. The availability, timeliness, and the costs involved in providing such information were simply assumed away. In this section we focus our attention on information systems. The "raison d'être" of information systems can be attributed to two essential functions (1) Reducing Uncertainty (2) Organizing Complexity. The first function, uncertainty reduction, presupposes that events occur randomly and that managers can make better decisions by reducing this randomness. For example, a production manager facing an uncertain demand for a product can develop more efficient production schedules if he can devise mechanisms which can reliably predict the demand. The quality of the predictions are then measured in terms of how well they replicate the actual demands. The better the predictions, the better the information system. Here, the "proof is in the pudding". In other words, the information system is evaluated a-posteriori in terms of the predictions and actual outcomes.

To reduce uncertainty, managers search, collect, accumulate, absorb, manipulate and transform data. The combination of these activities defines the information system. When the transformed data is used by the managers, they assume that it is a "deterministic equivalent representation" of the uncertain environment. In other words, the information system absorbs the uncertainty[11] inherent in the environment and replaces it by measures which are essentially deterministic and on the basis of which actions or descriptive statements of the system processes can be reached (see Figure III.13).

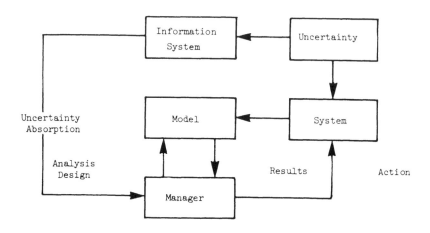

Figure III.13: The Absorption of Uncertainty by Managers

Uncertainty	Information System
Input	Forecast
Transformation Process	Functional representation and parameter identification
Output	Measurement

Figure III.14: Functions of Information Systems and Uncertainty Reduction

As discussed in section III.1 there may be uncertainty with respect to one or all of a system's components - input, transformation process and output. When an input is uncertain, the information system seeks to define <u>forecasts</u> of future inputs by using data, models and other mechanisms. When a transformation process is unknown the information system attempts alternative <u>parameters and functional representations</u> of the transformation processes and uses a given set of criteria to choose a particular representation. Finally, when the output is uncertain, the information system <u>measures</u> the output and replaces it by an <u>estimate</u> which is essentially a deterministic equivalent to the actual but uncertain output. Each of the problems we have indicated here is concerned with uncertainty reduction and is achieved by an appropriate use of statistical techniques.[12]

Information systems may also be devised to organize systems which have no uncertainty but are characterized by their complexity. For example, assume that a bank has a credit file on its customers and consider the request of a particular customer for a loan. The first step the bank manager might take is to check the customer's credit history by retrieving his credit file from a data bank. Given a large number of customers, how is the bank manager going to retrieve the file? While this problem is theoretically a simple one, in practice it is not. To obtain fast and efficient

access to the customer's file, an information system is required
which describes what procedures to follow in searching for the
file. Such an information system would reduce the complexity
of the data bank by replacing the whole data bank by a logical
construct of separate files. Although the importance of "complex"
information systems is great, we will essentially discuss here
the information systems concerned with uncertainty reduction.

The emerging importance of information systems as necessary
tools for the management of social and economic systems has
occurred with the simultaneous development of high-speed computers
which can efficiently handle large bodies of data. The combination
of data needs and requirements to comprehend and control increasingly
complex systems has led to an information revolution. Such a
revolution can be managed to the extent that we develop the
tools for discerning

> What information is relevant (both qualitatively and quantitatively)
>
> How often the information is required
>
> How it should be collected, processed and stored
>
> Where, when and how should data be relayed and displayed
>
> Who can get access to what type of data

In practice, the assessment of the costs and the
benefits of information is very difficult.

Such difficulties arise from the special attributes of information, the various meanings and uses of information, as well as technical difficulties in measuring the costs and benefits of information (even when information is well defined).

In information systems analysis and design[13], information is a resource. In other words, the utlity of information processes are evaluated in terms of their contribution to a system's performance. In this case, information is a valuable resource which can be substituted with control and physical resources in the attainment of organizational and economic goals. Here information is an economic resource having some of the following properties;

Its value is temporally dependent; the more "timely" the information the greater its value in use

It can be stored for future use, but the value and relevance of the information may depreciate over time

The repetitive imparting of information does not change its content. Thus, while information is a resource that can be used, it is not consumed[14]

The availability and selective imparting of information is a source of economic control and power.

The properties of information indicated prescribe that information, just as control, involves processes which require management. Furthermore, both decision making and information management can, in some cases be substitutes, that is they can be used as two means achieving the same end.

In decision theory [15], interest is given to the value in use of information. That is, information is evaluated in terms of its economic value. The questions we face then are to define measures or indices which can characterize the economic value of information and information systems. The value of information is as we indicated earlier, typically reflected in:

   (i) better forecasts (input uncertainty reduction)

   (ii) better identification (transformation process reduction)

   (iii) better measurements (output uncertainty reduction)

These estimates, ultimately used in the context of strategic or tactical actions contribute to the measures of a system's performance. Nonetheless, improved performance realized by information gathering and processing activities incurs costs. Thus, we can define the value of information and information systems as:

> The net benefits realized in system performance by introducing and maintaining an information system.

Figure III.6 summarizes how such benefits are computed and emphasizes the mean and variance of improved performance. In other words, the value of information and information systems is measured in terms of their influence on the expected values and risks of a system's performance. Computationally, the estimation of costs and benefits of information systems may be, except in very simple cases, a complicated matter. By simulation. however, the cost/benefit analysis of a complex information system may turn out to be procedurally simple. In Chapters V and VI we shall return to problems involving design of information systems. In particular optimal plans for the design of inventory monitoring plans will be given.

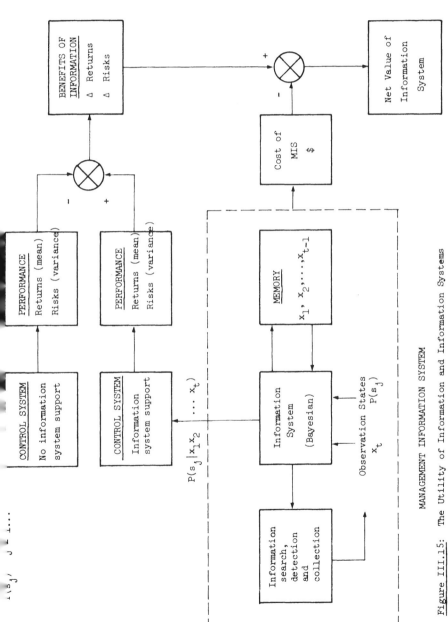

Figure III.15: The Utility of Information and Information Systems

III.5 The Choice of Decision Structures

We pointed out earlier that optimum control strategies consist in maintaining an acceptable or optimum level of performance. Such performance may be expressed in terms of degrees of stability, sensitivity, cost (or profits) and constraints on specific system trajectories. In practice, the choice of a decision procedure, may determine whether the implementation of a particular control study will be successful.[16] Managers are aware of and sensitive to decision procedures; furthermore, they often possess experience and intuition for which the solution of complex optimization problems on the basis of one (or a few) criterion cannot be an adequate substitute. A manager's decision procedure is laden with constraints which cannot always be included in a quantitative model. Therefore, if the solution of a particular control problem yields a decision procedure considered acceptable, the model is considered implementable. Otherwise, the model is considered a theoretical exercise. For example, the production model presented by Holt, Modigliani, Muth and Simon[17] is a successful case in which the solution--a linear feedback production decision rule deemed implementable--has led to acceptability of the model as a whole.

The criteria on the basis of which a decision procedure can be chosen are numerous. Some of these may be; (1) Limited complexity; this is a function of a manager's ability to deal with this complexity. (2) Inclusion of managerial practices and provision for a timetable for changing decision mechanisms. This timetable would involve management as an essential element of this change, in order to ensure the success of implementation.

(3) Careful support of a timely, economical and nonredundant information system. This consists in establishing a relevant information pattern and seeking procedure for compiling the information pattern to the actual decision - or, feedback control.

(4) Sensitivity to the environment and flexibility in meeting contingencies. These and other considerations provide a framework for investigating relevant and implementable decision procedures.

In searching for functional forms of control we may consider one of the following (Kleindorfer[18]):

(1) Closed-Loop or Feedback Controls - These are controls which were discussed earlier. In computing them, all the information available at the time of exercising the control is assumed to be used as a conditioning argument for the control laws.

(2) Open Loop, No Updating - Controls are conditioned only on initial information. Even if further information becomes available, these initially computed controls are enacted up to the end of a given planning horizon.

(3) Open Loop, Updating - Same as (2) except that controls are recomputed as new information becomes available.[19]

(4) Mean Value Approximations - In this approach, (consider a stochastic system's evolution) all random components are set equal to their expected value. Then the control law is computed for the resulting deterministic problem. This procedure may be used in either an updating or no updating version. It is of course only an approximation, except in one extremely important case - the unconstrained quadratic cost linear system case. There, control generated by (1), (2), (3) and (4) turn out to be the same. A solution by mean value approximation yields therefore the current best decision (see Witsenhausen [39] for further study of this problem and additional references).

(5) Best Within a Class - Here one uses qualitative information and insights about the form of the optimal law to deduce an interesting and easily parameterized class of control laws.[20] (e.g. linear in the present state, constrained to specific functional configurations such as step functions etc.).

The choice of any of the control approaches outlined above is a difficult one. In summary, we note that there are three functions we ought to consider; The structural form of the decision process (representing bias on the part of management, and acceptance of certain predetermined decision patterns); The informational base (or pattern) available for management decisions and; The implicit and explicit administrative costs in managing a particular decision procedure.

Decisions procedure may be suggested on the basis of past decision making behaviors, and the explicit management preferences for certain approaches to decision making (e.g. feedback versus non feedback).

Having described the implications of processes of time to management in Chapter I, the techniques and models for mathematically constructing the process of temporal change in Chapter II, and the essential decision-control problems in this chapter, we next turn our attention to the solution of these problems.

FOOTNOTES

1. See for example Klir and Valach (21), Bertalanffy (6), Ashby (5), Johnson, Kast and Rozensweig (18).

2. That is, subject to managerial control and internal to the system.

3. Under some managerial or other control which is not predetermined by the system trajectories. Therefore, such stimuli are inputs to that system.

4. This criterion consists in computing error estimates and minimizing the squared sum of these errors.

5. That is, prescribing what the functional forms of the probability distributions of ξ and η are.

6. See Cyert and March (10), Williamson (37).

7. See (7).

8. See Darwin (11), Rashevski (31). Specifically, the reader is referred to an outstanding discussion of these problems in Rosen (32).

9. Kurz (22, 23) suggested an application of the inverse control problem to economics. Mathematical developments concerning this problem have been suggested, however, by Douglas (12), Kalman (10), Jameson and Kreindler (17), Anderson (2), Anderson and Moore (3).

10. A system is termed controllable to some point $x_1 = a_1$, $x_2 = a_2 \ldots x_n = a_n$, if for each initial state, there exists a piecewise continuous control such that the point $(a_1 a_2 \ldots a_n)$ can be obtained in some finite time T. Thus, controllability merely indicates the possibility of reaching a set of points by control. This problem will be discussed further in Chapter IV.

11. The absorption of uncertainty is a term indicated by March and Simon (24) in the context of power and dominance.

12. In other words, a data set is replaced by one or a set of numbers representing the data set and to which we can associate levels of confidence.

13. Some references on information systems and their management are Marshak (25, 26, 27) Radner (29), and an extensive list of references in McGuire and Radner (28).

14. This is an important issue to which we cannot devote much attention.

15. See Raiffa and Schlaifer (30) and Winkler (38).

16. Problems of implementation have recently attracted the interest of management scientists. The essential premise of these studies is that to implement management decision programs, the scientist must be keenly aware of a manager's personality and behavior, as well as other factors having to do with the behaviors of people (see (8, 16, 36)).

17. See (15).

18. The classification below is based on an excellent survey by Kleindorfer (20). See also (36, 39).

19. See Dreyfus (13, 14) for a discussion of these three types of control.

20. In parts of the control literature this is also called specific control when it is applied to control problems and specific estimation when it is applied to estimation problems. For references on this problem, see (1, 9, 33 34, 35).

References

1. Agarwal, G. C. and R. Sridhar, Design of Specific Optimal Control Systems", *IEEE Region Six Conference Record*, 2, 1966, 717-726.

2. Anderson, B.D.O., "The Inverse Problem of Optimal Control," Report No. SEL-66-038 (Tr. No. 6560-3), Stanford Electronics Laboratories, Stanford, Cal., May 1966.

3. ─────── and J. B. Moore. *Linear Optimal Control*. Englewood Cliffs, N.J., Prentice Hall, 1967.

4. Arrow, K.J. and S. Karlin, "Production Over Time with Increasing Marginal Cost," in K.J. Arrow, S. Karlin and H. Scarf (Eds.). *Studies in the Mathematical Theory of Inventory and Production*, Chapter IV. Stanford, Cal., Stanford University Press, 1958.

5. Ashby, W.R., *Design for a Brain*. New York, Wiley, 1960.

6. Bertalanffy, L.V., *General System Theory*. New York, George Braziller, 1968.

7. Churchman, C.W., "On Rational Decision Making," *Management Technology*, 2, 1962, p. 71.

8. Churchman, C.W. and A.H. Scheinblatt, The Researcher and the Manager: A Dialectic of Implementation" *Management Science*, 11, 1965.

9. Cruz J.B., Jr., *Feedback Systems*, (Chapter 6), pp. 183-240), New York, McGraw Hill Book Co., 1972.

10. Cyert, R. and J.G. March, *A Behavioral Theory of the Firm*. Englewood Cliffs, New Jersey, Prentice Hall, 1963.

11. Darwin, C., *On the Origin of Species by Means of Natural Selection, or the Preservation of Favoured Races in the Struggle for Life*. London, Murray, 1859, 6th ed. 1878.

12. Douglas, J., "Solution of the Inverse Problem in the Calculus of Variations," *Transactions of the American Mathematical Society*, 50, 1941, pp. 71-128.

13. Dreyfus, S.E., Some Types of Optimal Control of Stochastic Systems, *J. SIAM on Control*, Ser. A, 2, 1964, 120-134.

14. Dreyfus, S.E., "Introduction to Stochastic Optimization and Control, in H. Darreman (Ed.) *Stochastic Optimization and Control*, New York, Wiley, 1968.

15. Holt, C., F. Modigliani, J.F. Muth and H.A. Simon, Planning Production, Inventories and Work Force, Englewood Cliffs, N.J. Prentice Hall, 1960.

16. Huymans, J.H.B.M., The Implementation of Operations Research, New York, Interscience, 1970.

17. Jameson, A. and E. Kreindler, "Inverse Problem of Linear Optimal Control," SIAM Journal on Control, 11, 1973, pp.

18. Johnson, R.A., F.E. Kast and J.E. Rosenzweig. The Theory of Management of Systems. New York, McGraw Hill Book Company, 3rd ed., 1973.

19. Kalman, R.E., "When is a Linear Control System Optimal?" Journal of Basic Engineering (ASME Tr.), 86, Series D, 1964.

20. Kleindorfer, P.R., "Stochastic Optimization of Dynamic Models", TIMS XX International Meeting, Tel-Aviv, Israel, June 1973.

21. Klir, J. and M. Valach. Cybernetic Modeling. Princeton, New Jersey, D. Van Nostrand, 1966.

22. Kurz, M., "The General Instability of a Class of Competitive Growth Processes," Review of Economic Studies, 35, 1968, pp. 155-174.

23. ———, "On the Inverse Problem," Lecture Notes in Operations Research and Mathematical Economics, Vol. 11, Mathematical Systems Theory and Economics, I. New York, Springer-Verlag, 1969.

24. March, J.G. and H.A. Simon. Organizations. New York, Wiley, 1964.

25. Marschak, J., "Economics of Inquiring, Communicating, Deciding," American Economic Review, Proc., 58, May 1968, pp. 1-18.

26. ———, "Economics of Information Systems," Journal of the American Statistical Association, 66, 1971, pp. 192-219.

27. ———, "Problems in Information Economics," in C. Bonini et al. (Eds.). Management Controls: New Directions in Basic Research. New York, McGraw Hill Book Company, 1971.

28. McGuire, C.B. and R. Radner (Eds.). Decision and Organization. A Volume in Honor of Jacob Marschak. Amsterdam, North Holland Publishing Company, 1972.

29. Radner, R., "Normative Theory of Individual Decision: An Introduction," in C.B. McGuire and R. Radner (Eds.). Decision and Organization. Amsterdam, North Hollan, 1972. pp. 1-18.

30. Raiffa, H. and R. Schlaifer. Applied Statistical Decision Theory. Cambridge, Mass., Division of Research, Graduate School of Business Administration Harvard University, 1961.

31. Rashevski, N., Mathematical Biology of Social Behavior. Chicago, University of Chicago Press, 1951.

32. Rosen, R., Optimality Principles in Biology. London, Butterworth, 1967.

33. Sage, A.P. and B.R. Eisenberg, Closed-Loop Optimization of Fixed Configuration Systems, International Journal of of Control, 3, 1966, 183-194.

34. Sims, C.S. and J.L. Melsa, "Specific Optimal Estimation", IEEE Transactions on Automatic Control, AC-14, 1969, 183-186.

35. Sims, C.S. and J.L. Melsa, "A Survey of Specific Optimal Techniques in Control and Estimation, International Journal of Control, 14, 1971, 299-308.

36. Tapiero, C.S., "Optimum-Constrained-Production Control," Working Paper, Hebrew University, 1975.

37. Williamson, O.E. The Economics of Discretionary Behavior: Managerial Objectives in a Theory of the Firm. Englewood Cliffs, New Jersey, Prentice Hall, 1964.

38. Winkler, R.L. An Introduction to Bayesian Inference and Decision. New York, Holt, Rinehart and Winston, 1972.

39. Witsenhausen, H.S., Separation of Estimation and Control for Discrete Time Systems, Proceedings of the IEEE, 59, 1971, 1557-1566.

Additional References

Ackoff, R.L., "Management Mis-Information Systems," *Management Science*, 14, 1967, B-147, B-156.

Ackoff, R.L., "Systems, Organizations and Interdisciplinary Research," *General Systems*, 5, 1960, 1-8.

Ackoff, R.L., "Towards a System of System Concepts," *Management Science*, 17, 1971, 661-671.

Argyris, C., "Management Information Systems: The Challenge to Rationality and Emotionality," *Management Science*, 7, 1971, 275-297.

Ashby, R.W., "General Systems Theory as a New Discipline," *General Systems*, 3, 1958, 1-6.

Ashby, R.W., "Requisite Variety and its Implications for the Control of Complex Systems," Second International Congress on Cybernetics, Namur 1950.

Bauer, R.A. (ed.), *Social Indicators*, Cambridge, Mass., M.I.T. Press 1966.

Bertalanffy, L.V., "General System Theory: A Critical Review," *General Systems*, 7, 1962, 1962, 1-20.

Carroll, D.C., "On the Structure of Operational Control Systems in J.F. Pierce Jr. (Ed.)," *Operations Research and the Design of Management Information Systems*, Technical Association of the Pulp and Paper Industry, TAPPI, 1967.

Cherry, C., *On Human Communication*, Wiley, 1957.

Churchman, C., *The Design of Inquiring Systems*, Basic Books, New York, 1971.

Crosson, F.J. & K.M. Sayre, (Eds.), *Philosophy and Cybernetics*, University of Notre Dame Press, 1967, Notre Dame London.

Farmer, J., "Management Control Systems," The Rand Corp., Santa Monica, California, June 1963.

Feltham, G.A., "The Value of Information," *The Accounting Review*, Vol. 43, 1968, 684-696.

George, F.H., "Automation Cybernetics and Society," Philosophical Library, New York, 1959.

Hall, A.D., R.E. Fagen, "Definition of System," *General Systems*, I, 1956, 18-29.

Hoos, Ida, R., "Information Systems and Public Planning," *Management Science*, 17, 1971, pp. 658-671.

Kitagawa, T., "Information Science and Its Connection with Statistics," *Proceedings* of the 5th Berkeley Symposium on Math. Statistica and Probability, Vol. I, Statistics by Lucien Le Lane and J. Neyman, UCLA Press, 1967.

Klir, G., "*An Approach to General Systems Theory*," New York, D. Van Nostrand, 1969.

Kriebel, C.H., "Operations Research in the Design of Management Information Systems," in J.F. Pierce Jr., (Ed.) *Operations Research and the Design of Management*, Information Systems, TAPPI, 1967, New York (Technical Association of the Pulp and Paper Industry).

Land, K.C., "Social Indicators in R.B. Smith (ed.)", *Social Science Methods*, New York Free Press, 1972.

Lewin, K.A., *A Dynamic Theory of Personality*, New York, McGraw Hill, 1935.

Lewin, K., *Field Theory in Social Science*, Edited by D. Cartwright, New York, Harper Torchbook, 1951.

Mesarovic, M.D., *Views on General Systems Theory*, Wiley, New York, 1964.

Newton, R.G., "Inverse Problems in Physics," *SIAM Review*, 12, 1970, 346-356.

Prince, T.R., "Information Systems for Planning and Control in J. Blood Jr. (Ed.)," *Management Science in Planning and Control*, TAPPI, STAP, No. 5, 1969, New York.

Rapoport, A., "Conceptualization of a System as a Mathematical Model in J.R. Lawrence (Ed.), *O.R. in Social Sciences*, London Tavistock, Publishing Co., 1966.

——————, "Mathematical Aspects of General Systems Theory," *General Systems*, 11, 1966, 3-11.

Rosenthall, R.A. and R.S. Weiss, "Problems of Organization Feedback Process," Ch. 5 in R.A. Bauer (Ed.) *Social Indicators*, Cambridge, Mass. M.I.T. Press 1966.

Sheldon, E.B. and W.E. Moore (Eds.), *Indicators for Social Change: Concepts and Meaurements*, New York, Russel Sage Foundation, 1968.

Simon, H.A., "The Architecture of Complexity," *General Systems*, 10, 1965, 63-76.

Simon, H.A., *The New Science of Management Decision*, New York, Harper & Row, 1960.

Strong, E.P. and R.D. Smith, *Management Control Models*, New York Holt Rinehart and Winston, 1968.

Tustin, A., *Mechanism of Economic Systems*, Cambridge, Mass., Harvard University Press, 1953.

Van Court Hare Jr., *Systems Analysis*, Harcourt Brace & World Inc. New York, 1967.

Wiener, N., *Cybernetics*, New York, Wiley, 1948.

Wiener, N., *The Human Use of Human Beings: Cybernetics and Society*, Avon Books, 1950.

Young, S., "Organization as a Total System," *California Management Review*, 10, 1968.

Yovitz, M.C., G.T. Jacoby & C.D. Goldstein (Eds.) *Self-Organizing Systems*, Spartan Books, Washington, D.C. 1962.

Problems

1. (i) Describe a business as an input-output model. What are the input variables (sources of uncertainty, environmental effects, managerial constraints and practices, managerial decision making) and what are the output variables (product quality, quantity, inventory, profits, costs etc.). What is a business state and how does the state relate to the output? (ii) Consider instead of a business, the administration of a city, a welfare agency.

2. Management control may be defined as those activities which are designed to compel events to conform to plans...It is thus the function that what is done will be that which is intended. For scientists, control is defined as a system or device which exerts a restraining, governing or directing influence. Compare these two approaches to control, what are the similarities? differences?

3. Describe as a feedback model the process of industry wages-prices-cost-of-living increases. Can you suggest some functional relationships between these variables? What kind of problems (i.e. identification, estimation, control etc.) would we encounter in such a model? How would you change your model if wages are also determined by the wage in other industries?

4. The simple lot-size inventory problem with inventory lot Q, constant demand rate s, h inventory storing cost per unit time, K set-up cost is resolved by minimizing the average total cost TC;

$$TC = Ks/Q + hQ/2$$

Show that this problem can be formulated as;

$$\text{Minimize } TC = \sum_{i=1}^{2} c_i x_i(T) \text{ subject to:}$$

$$dx_1(t)/dt = 1 \qquad x_1(0) = 0, \qquad c_1 = 0$$

$$dx_2(t)/dt = h(1-sx_1(t)/Q) + Ks/Q^2 \qquad x_2(0) = 0, \qquad c_2 = s$$

5. Numerous hypotheses have been suggested about the relationship between advertising, sales and their rates of change. In the most general formulation of the advertising problem we consider an optimization problem given by;

$$\text{Maximize } \int_0^T \exp(-rt)p(t)dt$$

$$\text{subject to} \qquad ds(t)/dt = g(a(t),s(t)) \qquad p(t) = f(a(t),s(t))$$

and initial conditions given. Here $a(t)$ = advertising rate at time t, $s(t)$ = sales at time t, $p(t)$ = profits at time t and r = discount rate, The specification of the response to advertising function g is a matter which is not agreed by all market researchers. (i) Can you suggest models (excluding those of Nerlove-Arrow and Vidale-Wolfe) of sales response to advertising (ii) What are the signs of the partial derivatives of the profit function (iii) What kind of control problems can we define (deterministic, stochastic, estimation).

6. The investment problem (how much to invest at time t to maximize the net present value of the investment in a planning time T) is based on the assumption that profits at time t are a function of capital goods; $p(t) = f(k(t))$, $p(t)$ = profits, $k(t)$ = capital stock. Assume a linear depreciation and a net investment i at t, $i = dk(t)/dt$. Gross investments are then given by: $I(t) = k(t) + dk(t)/dt$ while a net present value at t is
e $\exp(-rt)(p(t) - I(t))$ where r = discount rate. Formulate the optimum investment problem.

7. More data always lead to better results! Is this true? If yes, when and why? If not, when and why not?

8. Assume that "D" is a set of alternative decisions available to a decision maker. The elements of this set are $\{d_0, d_1, d_2, \ldots\}$. Let "S" be a set of states of nature. The elements of S are $\{s_0, s_1, s_2, \ldots\}$. The measurement of this state is given by a function $\eta(s)$; therefore a decision maker's observation is given by $y = \eta(s)$. If δ is the decision function, $d = \delta[\eta(s)]$ and if $\rho(s,d)$ is the outcome obtained if decision d is taken and state s turns out to be the state of nature, show that:

   a. Acts are defined by $a(s) = \rho\{s, \delta[\eta(s)]\}$
   b. The value of information is given by $c = \rho\{s, \delta[\eta(s)] - \gamma(n)\}$ where $\gamma(n)$ is the cost of information for each state s.
   c. If $u(\rho(s), \delta(s))$ is the utility of the outcome, show that the utility of the pair (η, δ) (i.e. the information measurement and decision strategies) is given by

   $$U(\eta, \delta) = \sum_{s \in S} \phi(s) u(s, \delta[\eta(s)])$$

   where $\phi(s)$ is the probability distribution of each of the states.

9. Establish a complete analogy between information management and production management. What are the differences? What are the similarities?

10. The value of information equals the market price -- discuss the implications of treating information as a commodity sold in a market.

11. Explain how you can improve management controls by a more timely availability of information. Structure your arguments in quantitative terms.

12. How would you establish criteria for information systems design?

13. What are the differences and similarities between data provided for
    a. evaluation purposes
    b. identification purposes
    c. decision making

14. How can you "plan" an information system and influence the expected outcomes? How objective can you be in designing an information monitoring program.

15. What is the usefulness of a computer in designing an information system? in monitoring a program?

16. Uncertainty concerning the functional form can be of three essential forms

    (a) Parameter uncertainty, i.e., a function $f(x,\theta)$ is known but its parameter θ is to be estimated

    (b) Uncertain functional structure, i.e., the function $f(x,\theta)$ is assumed to take on with a known (or unknown) probability distribution a set of function forms $f_i(x,\theta_i)$ $i = 1,\ldots,n$. Here the parameters θ_i are again unknown

    (c) Complete uncertainty, i.e., the functional form is unknown.

    In each of the cases above, how would you devise an information system which can improve over time your estimate of the functional forms and parameters?

17. The processes of problem solving and decision processes prescribe the information requirement - Discuss.